DITCHING THE SKY

A MEMOIR OF TRIUMPH AGAINST ALL ODDS

For Chick, Bob, Jim and Ernie
Gone West, but not forgotten

"When you see the Southern Cross for the first time,
you understand now why you came this way."

From the song "Southern Cross"
Lyrics by Stephen Stills, Rick Curtis, Michael Curtis

Review of *Ditching the Sky*

Retired airline pilot Porch tells the story of the harrowing day she had to land her plane in the middle of the Pacific Ocean.

On August 12, 1984, the oil pressure in the tiny four-seater that the author was ferrying to New Zealand started to fall slowly and inexplicably; when it hit zero, the engine failed. Luckily, when she was 17, Porch had learned to fly in engineless gliders. Now, more than a decade later, this saved her life, as she was able to maneuver her plane well enough to survive its crash into the sea. Much of Porch's story in this memoir involves catastrophic moments with unexpected saving graces…. Porch organizes her memoir smartly, interweaving memories of her childhood and early flying career with the immediate emergency of 1984, the day she "ditched" (a pilot's term for making an emergency landing and exiting a sinking aircraft). This back-and-forth can mean that some sections unnecessarily repeat details, but they do so for a reason: to bring readers back into the desperate situation in the cockpit….

A magnificent story of a woman who dealt with catastrophe with courage and humility.

—*Kirkus Reviews*

HEIDI A. PORCH

DITCHING THE SKY

A MEMOIR OF
TRIUMPH
AGAINST ALL ODDS

SONOMA, CA

Contents

One

Pacific Ocean
540 miles east northeast of Hawaii
August 12th, 1984
2:14 PM
Five hundred feet

"Okay, Heidi. Master Switch off. Good luck."

That would be the last radio transmission I would hear from Earl, my wingman, who was flying a Cessna 172 just off of my right wingtip.

I reached my hand out to the forward instrument panel of the Cessna 182, placed my finger over the toggle switch and hesitated. I knew that once I turned off the Master Switch, it would sever all electrical power to my radios. I would be cut off, unable to communicate with Earl, the crew of the Navy P-3 Orion, that was circling overhead, and to any other aircraft listening in on the emergency radio frequency. Gone would be any sense of comfort I had received from them. This went against my instincts. I desperately wanted to stay connected, but I knew I had no choice. It was the last item in an emergency procedure that had to be performed. I heard and felt the click from my fingertip pushing the Master Switch to the Off position. It was done.

The engine of my four-seater aircraft had failed minutes earlier. In the hours before, I had a warning that this might happen, but I kept hoping against hope that the engine would continue to run until I reached the coast of Hilo, Hawaii, over

500 miles off the nose. With all power lost, I was now, essentially, flying a heavy glider. I instantly reverted back to my experience as a young girl, flying gliders in the Bay Area of northern California. It felt natural, and I found some comfort in that. But what wasn't natural was that I was rapidly descending into the unknown. I could feel my heartbeats quicken with each foot of lost altitude.

Two hundred feet.

What had I forgotten? There was no one to ask now. I instinctively looked over to where Earl had been flying in formation with me, but I couldn't see him! He was gone! Logically, I knew that he must have moved further back into my five o'clock position, but it felt as though he had deserted me. I felt a pang of despair, but I couldn't give in to it. My training and experience had kicked in, and I knew I had to keep my emotions in check until after I hit the water. There would be time to fall apart later. I hoped.

Minutes earlier, I had opened the window and unlatched the door to my left, my only means of egress out of the airplane. I was worried that if the plane cartwheeled upon impact, the airplane fuselage might 'torque,' thereby making it impossible to open the door to get out. I envisioned being trapped, still alive, in a cockpit full of water. The possibility of that happening terrified me. I instinctively shuddered at the thought. I knew from past experience what it felt like to drown. I remembered the sting of water forcing its way through my nose and throat as I struggled to breathe.

I adjusted my position in the seat, and could feel the slight tug of the safety lanyard which was tied around my waist. The lanyard had been extended from underneath a flap on the side of my four-man life raft, which had been perched on top of the forward gas tank, where the co-pilot's seat would have normally been. This would give me a lifeline to the raft in case we got separated once I was in the water. Hopefully, the tether would not get tangled up on debris in the aftermath of the 'landing.' But I couldn't worry about that now. One thing at a time.

I took a deep breath in, exhaled as hard as I could and gave my shoulder harness and seat belt one last bone-crunching pull. I could not get them any tighter. Hopefully, they would secure me with enough stability to survive what would surely be a violent deceleration.

My biggest fear was surviving the impact. To put the odds in my favor, I had decided to put my packaged life raft in my lap to use as a sort of 'airbag.' I had grabbed the handle of the bundle, and pulled the raft clumsily down into my lap. It felt heavy upon my thighs. And in order to make enough room for the bundle to sit between my body and the control yoke, I had to slide my seat all the way back. Being 'height challenged' at five feet four inches, I could no longer reach the rudder pedals which gave me directional control to the left and right. What made matters worse was that I could no longer see over the nose of the airplane. How was I going to know how close I was to touching down if I was 'blind' looking forward through the windshield? This was worse than I imagined. I subconsciously blinked, hoping that would make my forward vision clearer. No. I could only look out the left side of the cockpit now in order to judge my landing flare. Not an ideal situation by any means.

I had discussed the finer points of ditching with my wing-man, and with the Navy pilots, who were experts at this sort of thing. They advised me that the safest maneuver to survive a ditching is to 'stall' the aircraft just before touching down. Stalling is the point at which the wing of the aircraft stops 'flying.' It gives you the slowest possible forward momentum. But it means something else. With no airflow over the wings, the control yoke is basically worthless. The ailerons would be useless. And it was imperative for me to keep the wings level. If the plane stalled prior to touching down, one wingtip could drop lower than the other, and the plane would cartwheel, possibly end over end. It was crucial that I maintain control due to the fact that the top edge of the forward gas tank was inches to the right of my head. If the plane cartwheeled, the side of my head could hit the edge of tank, and I could lose consciousness. By keeping the wings level, chances were that the plane would flip with forward momentum, all of the forces going forward in a straight line.

But these Navy guys were experts! Did I dare go against their advice and instructions? I had to trust my instincts. I was the only one flying this plane, the Pilot-In-Command. They had no idea that my ability to control how the airplane now maneuvered was severely diminished. I decided that I would not stall, and instead carry a few extra knots of airspeed so even though I had no more rudder control, I could still control the ailerons, keeping the wings level. I still had control over the elevator on the tail, so I knew from my experience in gliders, I could control my airspeed.

One hundred feet.

I could see the sun-sparkled reflections dancing off the surface of the water through the open space between the door to my left and the windshield. This sight caught me by surprise. How odd, I thought. In all of my time ferrying aircraft over the ocean, I had never seen the water this close, and without the filter of a 'bubble;' the glass of the windshield and windows. I could almost reach out and touch the water. Soon, I would.

I had always marveled at the beauty of the ocean, but now it appeared ominous. It was going to harm me, to consume me. To what degree I did not know. I could taste a sourness in my mouth.

This was getting real.

Fifty feet.

I gripped the control yoke with both hands a bit tighter, surprised that my palms weren't sweating. Why wasn't I silently screaming inside my head from fear? I was surprisingly calm. All of my concentration was focused on the next few seconds.

Airspeed 65 knots.

Twenty feet.

Even though I could not see immediately over the nose, I could look out to the horizon. The swells were light, about two feet, but still not the flat surface needed for a controlled touchdown.

'I wonder what it is going to feel like?'

'It.' What a small word to represent such a massive meaning. '*It*' encompassed all of the unknown possibilities I was facing and imagining.

I had heard that when faced with impending catastrophe, your life flashes in front of your eyes. No. For me, my visions moved towards the future, not the past. What would take place in the next few seconds? What would *it* feel like should the plane break apart? Would I survive the ditching, but have my neck broken? What would *it* feel like if my ribs cracked, or if my body got lacerated from the ripped metal of the door, or the broken glass from a shattered windshield? What does *it* feel like to lose consciousness and drown, or even worse, be trapped inside the crippled airplane as it sinks below the surface? The 'best' case, and the 'worse' case might be a sudden jolt, and then permanent oblivion.

Five feet. Sixty-three knots.

Impact.

Two

I was five years old. Our family had just come back from my first real vacation; flying back to Detroit, Michigan from Hayward, California, to visit my grandparents. It had been my first experience on an airliner. But I wasn't new to the excitement of flying. My father owned a single-engine Cessna 170. It was beautiful. It had a pale blue, white and silver paint scheme with white leather upholstery. Dad and I would go flying most weekends, and I would sit upon three, thick phone books, so I could at least see out the windows.

Ever since I could walk, I became an 'airport bum.' I loved going out to the airport with Dad. There was such comradery with the other pilots that would be spending their weekends polishing their own airplanes; the mechanics, smelling of gasoline and oil, in their worn white overalls. I felt like 'one of the boys' when I was in their company.

But this 'airline' thing was totally different. An air of excitement hit me when I glanced into the cockpit while boarding, seeing all the dials and gauges and switches; the pilots in their sharp uniforms, gold and black epaulets proudly accentuating their shoulders. The 'stewardesses' (you could call them that back then) so friendly and pretty in their matching outfits, shiny wings on their lapels.

I can still remember being pushed back into my seat on takeoff. It was beyond thrilling. I was lucky enough to have been given the window seat, over the desires of my two older sisters. I couldn't believe how fast the earth was falling away. This was heaven, and a lot more exciting than the gentle ascent of the Cessna.

Age 3, Cessna 195, Oakland Airport

The cabin service began. You mean we get food on this airplane, as if the excitement of the flight wasn't enough? And some people were even getting wine! How elegant!

With the meal service nearly over, the lead stewardess came up to my sisters and me and asked us if we would like to help them collect the dinner trays. In return we would become 'official junior stewardesses' with a set of wings and an official ID card, commemorating the event! Heck, yeah! Even though I was very shy and nervous about taking the dinner trays away from passengers who were utter strangers to me, I couldn't pass up the chance at becoming an 'Official American Airlines Junior Stewardess!' It would be the highlight of my life!

As I made my way up and down the aisle, I could see a sudden glare of sunlight coming from the front of the airplane. The cockpit door was open, and the captain had come out to have a cup of coffee in the forward galley. One of the stewardesses went into the cockpit with a cup of coffee for the co-pilot and closed the door. I so wanted to go upfront and talk to the captain; to ask him what it was like to fly this amazing machine, but being painfully shy, I couldn't.

When we got back home, after spending two weeks with our grandparents, I was playing in the front yard when my neighbor, Mr. Mumma, came over to chat with me. He was the father of my buddy, Paul.

"So, how was your vacation, Heidi? Did you have fun?"

"Oh, yes." And I regaled him with my adventures.

"So, Heidi. What do you want to be when you grow up?"

"I want to be a *stewardess!*"

"And why is that?"

"'Cuz' you get to serve drinks and food, and pick up the trays, and you get to drive the airplane, and see lots of different places!"

"*Drive* the airplane?"

"Yeah. They all get to take turns. I saw them going in and out of the cockpit."

"No, Heidi. Only the pilots get to fly the plane."

"Oh," as I slowly took this in. "Then, I want to be an airline pilot."

And that was that. No need for further consideration or discussion. One day, I *was* going to be an airline pilot.

Three

The Plan

B ut, how to get there?
Most pilots wanting to fly for the airlines enlisted in the military. But that was not an option for me. By the time I finished high school, the only branch of the military that offered pilot positions for women was in helicopters. I needed fixed-wing experience. And if I was going to go the military route, I would have wanted to join the Navy, like my father did. Unfortunately, his color-blindness prevented him from flying in the military, but that had been his dream. So, he got his pilot's license during his off-duty time.

But I had a plan. I would get my Private Pilots license, my Commercial Pilots license, my Instructor license, teach flying to others, then get a Multi-Engine license, get a job flying for a small commuter airline, and then 'Voila!' I'm an airline pilot. Easy.

But life has other ideas.

All through my years in high school, I thought it very strange that my peers and friends had no idea what they wanted to do with their lives once they got into college and after. I thought that I was the norm, not the 'odd ball.' But I soon learned that I was cut from a different cloth. I'm sure that my friends and family thought that it was a phase I was going through; something I would grow out of eventually. And even though my parents supported my dream wholeheartedly, they still shared their concerns for me to have something to fall back on just in case some outside force prevented me from being able to fly. And let's face it, in those days women just *did not* fly for the airlines.

I developed an affinity towards drafting. I liked the precision of it all. I liked how you could have an idea of a structure, and then make it a reality, just by putting it down on paper. As soon as drafting classes were offered in high school, I quickly signed up, always being the only girl in the class. By the time I was halfway through my senior year, I had finished all the class assignments, and so I was made teacher's assistant. The skills I learned carried over in later years of my life. I designed all three of the houses in which I lived; each one a different style and character.

In the summer of 1973, the 'journey' began. I was given a gift certificate for an introductory lesson at the glider port in Vacaville, California. We had driven past the glider port many times on the way to my grandparents' house. The runway paralleled the freeway, and I marveled at how graceful the gliders appeared, floating just above the runway as the towplane they were tethered to built up enough speed to lift off. Then off they would ascend together until reaching an altitude where the glider would break its bond and be able to glide free.

My first lesson was in a Schweizer 2-33, a German-built training glider. It sat two, the student up front underneath a bubble canopy, with the instructor behind. I was nervous, excited and did not know what to expect. My only experience flying up to that point had been in my father's Cessna 170, but that had been sold when I was seven years old. This was my first real time at the controls of a 'flying machine.' I really couldn't count the time in the Cessna, as my legs were too short to reach the rudder pedals, and I wasn't tall enough to see over the nose. But as we lifted off on that first glider flight the sensation of being in the air again came rushing back. It was the same as before… pure bliss.

We reached an altitude, around 2,500 feet, where we could release the tow rope by pulling on a red ball on the instrument panel in front of me. The instructor told me to pull it, and when

I did, there was a very loud BANG! It sounded as if someone had taken a sledgehammer and hit the nose of the glider. We immediately pulled into a climbing right turn as the towplane pilot banked into a left descending turn, thereby avoiding the towrope that was whipping through the air.

Instantly, all I could hear was the gentle sound of the wind flowing over the wing surfaces. And then I heard the words, "Okay, Heidi. You've got it." He didn't have to say it twice. I gingerly took hold of the stick in my right hand and followed his instructions. I learned quickly that even though there was no engine, you could easily control the airspeed by how far you pushed the stick forward or back. By the time I was able to solo, I would be able to determine my exact airspeed, to within one or two knots, just by the noise of the air rushing past. We slowly made our way over to a small ridge that was on the east side of the airfield. The prevailing wind was from the west, which meant that as the wind approached the sloping ridge, it would travel up the slope, over the top to the downward sloping side. This upward moving air provided enough lift to support the weight of the glider and not lose any altitude. We flew back and forth just beneath the ridgeline joining a golden eagle who was either searching for prey or trying to figure out what this monstrosity of a bird was that had joined him.

And then it was time to return for a landing. I knew well before we touched down that I was hooked. And while I had never imagined starting my flying education in sailplanes, it was good fortune, to say the least. I feel that it made me an overall better pilot, more attuned to the basics.

I was able to take two more lessons in Vacaville but discovered that there was another glider port a bit closer to where I lived in the Bay Area, Sky Sailing Airport in Fremont, California.

What was even better, was that I could work part-time at Sky Sailing, thereby getting my lessons for nearly free.

The friends I made at Sky Sailing are friends I still have today. I was the 'little sister' to most of them, and they not only mentored me, but they also teased me relentlessly. I enjoyed every minute.

Schweizer 2-33 glider lesson, Sky Sailing glider port

Landing approach, Vacaville glider port

Throughout the next two years, I slowly accumulated enough flight hours to earn my private and then a commercial glider rating. This allowed me to give rides for hire, which really helped with the expenses of flying on my own. But I couldn't help but feel an overriding impatience to get busy on flying real airplanes. I was jealous of the tow plane pilots, and would bum rides off one of the lead tow pilots, John Painter, whenever I had the chance.

In 1975, my family ended up moving from California to Cedar Rapids, Iowa, due to a change in my father's employment. I had graduated from high school the previous year and had been working at Sky Sailing to save some money for college. My desire was to attend San Jose State University, which was one of the only schools that offered a degree in aviation. But, as much as my parents wanted to contribute to my college tuition, they were just not able to offer anything but moral support. So, in an effort to economize, I decided to join my parents in Iowa, and take some classes at the junior college that would transfer to San Jose later. I could always apply for scholarships and grants.

Leaving my pals at Sky Sailing was extremely difficult. They had taken me under their 'wings.' I was going to miss them terribly. The last day I worked at Sky Sailing, one of my pilot 'brothers,' Ken Couche, handed me an envelope. In it was a poem he had written about the comradery between pilots, and the joy of flight. At the bottom of the poem was a note that read, "To one who has shown us the way it can be." I will cherish it forever.

Strong and proud they were
who flew over the earth,
sharing with birds
and butterflies
the freedom of God,
I remember the spirit of those aviators,
their reminiscences of adventure

and the memory of a life of love
shared in their company.
It was the communion of animate
and inanimate,
of outspread wings and air—
a delicate celestial consummation.
It was the best I have ever known.

To one who has shown us the way it can be. Stay good!

Once in Cedar Rapids, I looked for a job; preferably anything at an airport, just to be close to the flying environment. What I ended up with was a job with the Cedar Rapids Airport security staff. In the mid 70's, there were no such things as x-ray machines for screening passenger carry-on bags. The only machinery we had were the walk-through metal detectors, which meant that all carry-on bags had to be physically opened and inspected for prohibited items. Not the most glamorous job, but hey... I was at the airport! And it paid not only for tuition at the junior college, but I was able to start taking real, honest-to-God flying lessons.

It was required that we have an off-duty policeman in the screening area for each outbound flight, in case we discovered a firearm in someone's bag, or other illegal substances. I got to know them pretty well in the quiet times between airline departures. Two of the officers flew the police department helicopters. It wasn't long before I was given permission to fly along with them on patrols. They let me work the spotlight, and we'd play 'spotlight tag' with some of the squad cars below. Unfortunately, my time aloft with them was suspended when we landed in the back lot of a pizza parlor to get some 'take out.'

Taking flying lessons in the Midwest, while not as picturesque as the varied landscapes of the San Francisco Bay Area with the Pacific Ocean, mountains, small towns, big cities, and vast areas of agriculture, flying around Iowa did prove to challenge your navigational abilities. Iowa was dotted with hundreds of small towns, most with a railroad track bisecting its borders and each with a water tower, boasting the name of the town. Flying a cross-country trip required attention to the smallest detail on the aeronautical chart. Did the railroad track take on a 30-degree bend to the north of the town, or was it closer to 45-degrees? What is that little lake doing there? I don't see it on the map. And flying down close enough to read the name of the town on the water tower was cheating! The only thing you could count on was that if you flew too far to the east, you'd cross the Mississippi River, and then you knew you went too far. I became very good at reading maps.

My flight instructor had his own challenges where I was concerned. He had never had a student before who already had a glider rating before starting their airplane training. He would often comment that my flying was smooth and precise. I couldn't wait until I would finally get to fly solo. So, when my instructor called me into his office for a 'chat,' I knew that he was going to give me the good news that my next flight would be my solo flight. My Dad would be so proud.

"Heidi, I really want to solo you, but frankly, I'm a bit worried."

This comment made me sick to my stomach. It was the last thing I was expecting to hear. Was I no good? Was this the end of my journey towards someday flying for the airlines? I thought I was doing okay, but could I be wrong? How was I going to break the news to my Dad?

He must have seen the confusion and disappointment on my face, and quickly explained.

"Heidi, in all our flights together, you have never had to abandon an approach to landing. You have never had to go-around because you were either too high, too low, too fast, or too slow. If you get into trouble, I don't know how you will handle it."

I explained to him that when you fly gliders, you don't get a second chance at a landing. You must make every approach one in which you can land. There is no engine to bail you out of a botched approach.

He mulled this over, and then slowly a grin appeared on his face.

"You solo tomorrow."

Four

Back to California

The avionics industry during the 70's and 80's was tumultuous, and in 1978, much to my delight, my father, who was an avionics engineer, decided to start his own business back 'home,' in Vacaville, California.

It was almost as if I had never left. I continued my flight training at the Nut Tree Airport, working towards my commercial and instrument ratings. At the same time, I got a job at the Vacaville Glider Port, where it all started, as the receptionist, answering phone calls, scheduling students, and selling rides. My duties also required that I 'run the line,' which meant that I would hook up the gliders to the end of the tow rope, and run alongside, holding a wingtip during the first few seconds of the takeoff roll until enough air flowed over the wing that the pilot could keep the wings level for the remainder of the takeoff. Occasionally, I would pilot the glider rides myself. But my real goal was to someday fly the towplanes.

Unfortunately, the owner of the operation wasn't too keen on having a girl piloting one of his towplanes. He didn't think girls had the stamina to spend all day sitting in a towplane, making 20 to 30 landings a day with hardly any time to break for food, or even go to the bathroom. And everyone knew that boys were better pilots, right? I suppose I should have been more appalled at the prejudice back then, but that was the way things were.

One of the 'regulars' at the glider port was a retired airline pilot. His name was Ernie Hummel. He was my friend, my mentor, and like a second father. He kept his own airplane, an open-cockpit Great Lakes biplane, hangered at the glider port. He would often take me up at the end of the day and give me aerobatic lessons. He taught me the intricacies of flying a tail-dragger airplane, and how it differs from conventional 'tricycle' gear airplanes. Flying an airplane with a wheel attached to the tail could prove extremely challenging, especially in strong crosswinds. You always ran the risk of ground-looping if you weren't on top of your game.

On most weekends, after we shut down for the day, he and I would sit on a log near the runway and share a bottle of cheap 'champagne' out of paper cups. We would discuss my dreams and my plans for the future. He knew how badly I wanted to fly the towplanes and get out of the office.

On one of those idyllic afternoons, he told me to meet him at the glider port the next morning about 30 minutes before my normal report time. He was going to change the oil on one of the towplanes as a favor to the mechanic and told me that I could warm up the engine by doing a couple of 'touch and goes' first. Anxious for any flight hours I could get, I got to the airport an hour early to clean the windshield, fuel up the plane and do a thorough preflight. I wanted everything ready before Ernie got there.

By the time Ernie arrived, the plane was set to go.

"Go ahead, Heidi. Take it around the patch two or three times."

"Aren't you going with me, Ernie?"

"Nope. I want to finish my coffee. You go ahead."

I jumped up into the cockpit of the Bellanca Scout, a fabric-covered blue and yellow taildragger; one of the two towplanes that we used for much of our towing. As I started the takeoff roll, I thought I noticed a man standing next to Ernie, near the office. It was probably just someone driving by that wanted a glider ride. But I couldn't dwell on that. I had to concentrate on my flying.

There was a healthy crosswind that morning, and so I decided to practice a landing technique that Ernie had taught me, a wheel landing. This entailed landing on the two main tires and keeping the tail wheel a few feet off the runway surface upon touchdown. As the groundspeed decreases, you gently bring the tail wheel down. I alternated each landing between a wheel landing and a three-point landing, landing on all three wheels at the same time. Even though Ernie told me to only take it around the pattern two to three times, I thought he wouldn't mind one extra landing, just to practice with the crosswinds.

As I taxied over to park in front of the hangar, I recognized the man who was still standing next to Ernie. It was Dave, the owner of the glider port. Unbeknownst to me, Ernie had asked Dave to meet him that morning. He wanted Dave to evaluate my landings and give me a job flying the towplanes. And when Dave told me that I could start towing full-time, I had to turn my head to hide the tears of gratitude and affection I had for Ernie.

Bellanca Scout towplane

I was persistent in my efforts to fly the towplanes full-time and get out of the office. My efforts eventually paid off, and I became one of the regular tow pilots, flying not only the Bellanca Scouts, but other models of taildraggers and towplanes. At the same time, I was continuing my education by working towards achieving my multi-engine and ATP (Airline Transport Pilot) ratings. The progress was slow, as lessons were very expensive, and I wasn't making much money towing gliders. I also knew that to get hired at an airline I would need a four-year college degree, and I had only finished two years of junior college so far.

And then, one day I heard about a ferry company, Transair, that had moved from Oakland Airport to the Nut Tree Airport.

Hmm. I couldn't help but wonder if they might consider hiring a low-time pilot, and a girl pilot at that. I spent the next few days working up the courage and practicing my 'pitch' to present to the owners of Transair.

Five

Transair, Inc.

I did a little research and discovered that Transair was in the business of ferrying airplanes, most of them single-engine Cessna airplanes right out of the factories in Wichita, Kansas, out to California, where they would be outfitted with extra gas tanks, and the radio equipment needed to fly them throughout the Pacific, mostly Hawaii, Fiji, New Zealand, and Australia.

I had heard that in order to get hired as a ferry pilot, Transair required 750 to 1000 hours of flight time. I only had around 500. I needed more flight time. But, no guts, no glory, right? I went into the Transair office one morning and asked to speak to the owners. I met Bruce, one of the two owners of the company and pled my case. I explained to him that I realized that I was short of hours to become one of their full-time ferry pilots, but if they ever needed a spur-of-the-moment pilot to help them pick up a plane in Wichita, and fly it back to California, to please call me. I kept worrying that they could sense the desperation in my voice. I really wanted this job!

It paid off. About a month later, I got a call from Earl, the other owner of Transair, who also did a lot of the flying, explaining that they had six airplanes to pick up in Wichita, and only had five pilots. He emphasized the fact that this was not an official job offer. But they were in a bind, and had no one else to call. Could I be ready to leave the next morning? Silly question.

Usually, the drill was to fly on a commercial airliner from

San Francisco, to Wichita, spend the night, and then depart early the next morning from the Cessna factory for the flight back to the Nut Tree Airport. But on this trip, they needed to return a Cessna 404, a multi-engine airplane back to the Cessna factory for some maintenance. It was just the right sized airplane to take all six of us back to Kansas.

I showed up, what I thought, was early for our departure. I was surprised to find that everyone was already onboard the 404 ready to go. As I entered the cabin and was about to introduce myself to the other pilots, a booming voice came from the cockpit.

"Hello Sugar-Bugar!"

Sugar-Bugar? Sugar-Bugar? How was I supposed to take that? As an endearment? As an insult?

The voice belonged to Bob Grantham, one of Transair's most senior ferry pilots. There was a slight Midwest twang to his accent, and a smile as big as the sky. I took an immediate liking to him. Little did I know that he would become a friend, a mentor, and eventually someone I would love.

"Take a seat," and he pointed to the co-pilot's chair.

Me? Sit in the pilot's seat? I had fully expected to sit quietly in the aft cabin, mind my own business and try to soak in the workings of ferry flying from the other pilots. I was not expecting to be put on the spot by flying a plane I had never flown before, and a more sophisticated twin-engine plane at that.

I climbed into the copilot's seat, buckled up, got my headset secured, took a scan of the instrument and radio panels, assuming that I would only be in charge of handling the radio calls for our flight, and nodded to Bob that I was ready.

"Okay, Heidi… she's all yours."

What? Me? With everyone watching? Up until that point, I only had about eight hours behind the controls of a multi-engine aircraft, and that was from a two-day multi-engine school I went to for my rating. Half of that time was spent 'flying' a multi-engine table-top simulator. The other four hours was in a very forgiving and basic airplane. The Cessna 404 was much more sophisticated and complex. But flight time was flight time and getting multi-engine experience was everything.

I hesitantly placed my left hand over the two throttle levers, and advanced them slowly. What I expected was for the airplane to slowly accelerate while tracking the centerline of the runway. But much to my utter humiliation, the plane quickly veered off towards the left side of the runway. Bob quickly took control, retarding the throttles and positioning the airplane back to the runway centerline.

I couldn't help but look behind me to see that all four pilots were leaning towards the center aisle looking at me with expressions on their faces of concern, exasperation, and amusement. I could have died from embarrassment. I fully expected Earl to say, "Stop everything! Heidi is getting out."

"This plane has a lot more power than you're probably used to, right?" And Bob winked at me.

Bob gave me a few pointers, and the second attempt went normally. Once we were up in the air, I found my comfort zone and was able to enjoy the four-hour flight to a fuel stop in Pueblo, Colorado. I flew the next leg onto Wichita uneventfully. My nerves calmed down when I glanced back into the cabin to see that everyone was asleep.

Over dinner and drinks that night at the hotel it was decided that I would be paired up with Earl for the two-day ferry flight back to Vacaville, laying over in Pueblo, Colorado, before crossing the Rockies the following day. Earl and I would each be flying Cessna 172-RGs, a four-seater airplane with a retractable landing gear. The other four airplanes varied in performance and speed. One of them would make the flight back to Vacaville in one day, but the rest of us would fly as a group.

The flight from Wichita to Pueblo was a learning experience. Earl explained to me that since these were brand new airplanes, some with only 20 minutes of flight time, they needed to be 'flown hard' on the way to California. The biggest concern, of course, was to break in the engines properly. This entailed keeping at least 75% power on the engine. The high temperatures would ensure that the piston rings would seat properly. Aside from the engine, we would operate every system on the aircraft; communications, navigational instruments, anti-ice, electrical, and ventilation components. Since these planes would be flying for many hours over open water, it was important to find out if something was not working correctly. If something was going to break, we wanted it to break over land. That meant keeping near maximum power on the engines on the flight to California. In order to do that, we kept our altitudes fairly low. This, of course, proved great fun when flying over open spaces. It also proved a little nerve wracking. If the engine did 'hiccup,' you wouldn't have much time to get your act together to find a suitable landing spot.

The next day proved a bit more challenging. Our flight plan had us depart Pueblo, Colorado, traverse the Rockies, and make a fuel stop in Milford, Utah, which was an unattended airport, with little to no services. If you needed help fueling your airplane, you would pick up the wall phone in the shed, call Lillian, who lived down the road, and she would come to help you.

The weather was supposed to be good enough for our time flying over the Rockies, but forecasts are not exact, at least they weren't back then. As we started our trek into the mountainous area, the clouds above us started getting lower and lower and lower. My anxiety went up and up and up. Many a pilot has gotten trapped in mountain canyons when the clouds rolled in unexpectantly, obscuring the mountain tops to where the pilot has no way of finding an exit route, and they crash into the terrain. I could tell from listening to the radio chatter from the other pilots that they were concerned about this too.

And then I heard Earl over the radio. "Heidi, you take the lead. If you can get us to Milford, you've got a job."

That was all the encouragement I needed. The elation I felt at getting a job offer overcame the trepidation I felt from the deteriorating weather. I guess the planets were in alignment for me that day, and with some creative changes in altitude and headings, I was able to lead us out of the unforgiving canyons, and break into the clear, just a few miles away from Milford. I was emotionally exhausted but elated.

Earl was good to his word, and when we got back to the Nut Tree, he reiterated his offer of a full-time position as a ferry pilot. I had but one stipulation.

"Earl, I will do all the domestic ferry flights you want, but if you think I am going to fly a single-engine airplane over the ocean, you're nuts!"

He smiled and said, "Deal."

Over the course of the next six months, I made 30 domestic ferry flights, mostly from Kansas to California, but some to Oregon, Oklahoma, and southern California. I flew nearly every model of single-engine Cessnas built, from 152s, little two place models, all the way up to the Cessna 210, a fast, high-performance airplane with all the bells and whistles. I flew the light twins, as well; 402s, 404s, 303s, and 414s. This was invaluable experience. Most pilots, after getting their instrument and commercial ratings, become flight instructors which is great experience. But I was selfish. I was the one that wanted to be behind the controls, and not let the students have all the fun.

Many of the ferry flights required several airplanes to be picked up at the same time. These flights were my favorite. I loved being 'one of the guys,' listening to their stories about their latest over-water trips, hearing about places like Hawaii, Pago Pago, Fiji, Norfolk Island, a small island colony near Australia where descendants of the Bounty mutineers live.

I had always had a fascination with World War II, and the battles in the Pacific. I wanted to have my own stories. So, one day, I went to Bruce and Earl and told them that I would like to try an ocean ferry to Sydney, Australia. But just ONE; just to say that I'd done it. I fully expected that after doing one international ferry flight, I could check that off my 'list,' and concentrate solely on domestic flights.

In March of 1982, I got my wish. I was assigned to fly a Cessna 206, a larger single-engine airplane that could hold six passengers, with a large cargo pod installed under the belly. I would be paired up with Bob, as my wingman, or as he was known throughout the Pacific, Rubberduck. He was awarded this nickname when on his first overwater flight, he showed up at the hangar with an inflatable rubber duck around his waist, and well, the name stuck. Soon after Bob was awarded his nickname, he began carrying a 'rubber duckie,' the kind that are sold as bath toys, with him on all of his flights. At the completion of each delivery, he would write a tally mark on the underside of the duck, whom he named Homer. Homer became one of our most important crewmembers.

First ocean crossing, Cessna 206

On our return flights from Australia to San Francisco, we would fly on Pan Am Airlines. If the 'gods' were with us, we would get upgraded to first class. Of course, this had nothing to do with the fact that we would buy two-dollar liters of vodka or gin in Pago Pago, and then Homer would gift them to the Pan Am ticket agents in Sydney. If there were open seats available, he would get an upgrade to first class with the stipulation that he could bring his team with him. Homer would be placed on the top of the seat backrest, and it didn't take long until the flight attendants became acquainted with him, and looked forward to spoiling him with the best cuts of prime rib for dinner, after dinner cordials, extra pillows, and anything else he desired.

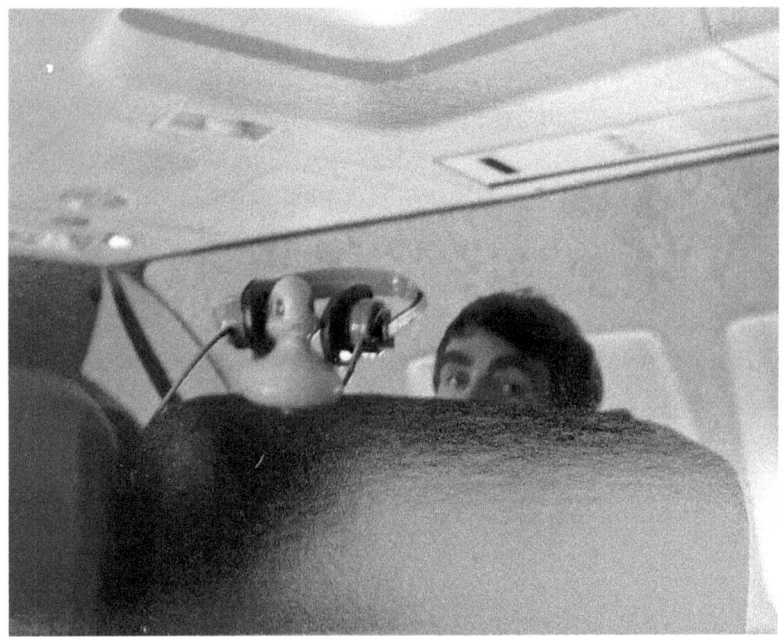

Jim York and Homer, Pan Am first class

On this first overwater trip, there would be a total of four airplanes, two of them with Sydney as their destination, and Bob and I flying to Brisbane, Australia. So, we would fly much of the trip as a group.

Tradition had it that on your first overwater ferry flight, one of the senior pilots would 'babysit' you, keeping an eye on you, teaching you the ropes, but mostly keeping you out of trouble. In the past, there had been some pilots on their first flight that once the sun came up on the first leg from California to Hawaii, would see the expanse of water that lay ahead of them, no land in sight, and have a panic attack. Their partner would either have to calm them down in order to continue, or they would have to turn around and be escorted back to the California coast. But, if you made it all the way to your final destination, you would pay your mentor $250 because they earned every penny!

I was told many times that a pilot would either love it or hate it. There was no in-between.

I absolutely loved it.

It wasn't just the excitement of seeing new places and people. There was something almost spiritual about knowing that you were the only person out there for hundreds of miles. The appearance of the ocean's surface would constantly change. One minute it would sparkle gold under hundreds of individual creamy white clouds, and then an hour later it might appear slate gray, the white caps dotting the tops of the waves like snow. I never got tired of watching the changes that would appear to me. But, without a doubt, the most beautiful sight I have ever witnessed in my years of flying was the first time I saw an ocean moonrise.

Pacific Ocean scenery

I was on a flight from Honolulu to Pago Pago (American Samoa). It was a crystal-clear night, and the stars were as plentiful as I had ever seen. I turned the lights down on my instrument panel to appreciate them fully. Way off in the distance, on the horizon was a line of cumulonimbus clouds. What caught my attention was that they were flickering from internal flashes of lightning. But after a few minutes, it seemed that the entire expanse of clouds was lit from within, glowing softly. As the light got brighter, it seemed as though someone had painted the edges of the clouds in liquid mercury. I was mesmerized. This only lasted a short time, because suddenly the top of the moon popped through the top of the clouds, and instantly a 'highway' of crushed diamonds laid out towards me from the light of the moon. I gasped at the sight of it. I had never seen anything before that literally took my breath away. To this day, whenever I see a moonrise, I think back to that flight and how lucky I was to see something that incredible.

Pacific Ocean scenery

Over the course of the next few trips, I learned about the 'gotchas' of navigation. Currently, with GPS, Global Positioning System that uses satellite technology, aircraft can navigate to within a mile, or less, of their desired course. But in the early 80's the only thing available to us for navigation was a LORAN-C, which was a medium range radio navigation system using land-based radio beacons. And the LORAN was only available on the first leg of an ocean flight, between California and Hawaii, approximately 2400 miles. After that, on the longer flight from Hawaii to American Samoa, approximately 2600 miles, the LORAN was only good for the first 600 miles.

For the majority of the ferry flights, navigation was done by 'dead reckoning,' calculating your airspeed, compass heading, time, and distance. The LORAN could get you to within 20-30 miles of your destination, on a good day. With dead reckoning, all bets were off. It depended upon how accurate your wind forecast was, how good you were at holding a constant heading in a plane that was often without an autopilot, and airspeed, and how talented you were at interpreting the direction the white caps would break to determine whether, or not, you needed to make a heading correction.

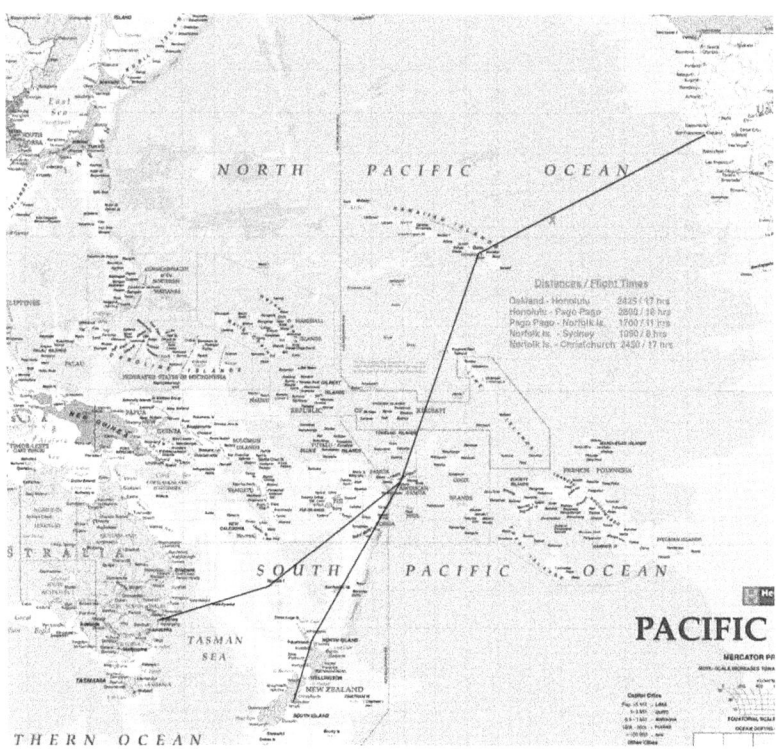

Typical route of flight, California to Australia/New Zealand

The first leg from the mainland to Hawaii is the longest

stretch of open water between two points of land in the world, approximately 2400 miles and 16 to 18 hours of flight time, which meant that if you encountered any problems, be it mechanical, or more commonly, the headwinds turned out to be stronger than anticipated, and you could risk running out of fuel. Your only choices were to continue on to Hawaii, or turn around and go back to California. On this leg we would take advantage of airliners flying overhead on their way from Hawaii into San Francisco. When they were directly overhead, we would ask them for the coordinates of their position and compare them to what our own calculations showed for our position, and be able to determine if we were falling behind, or on schedule.

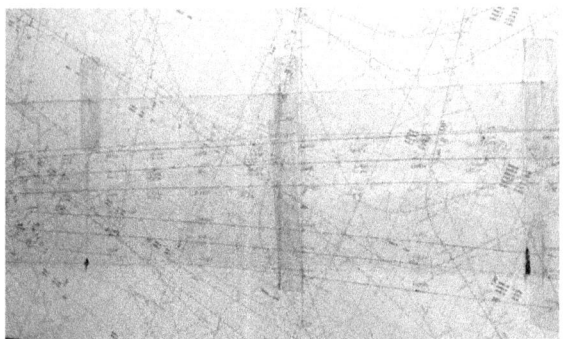

LORAN chart with airways between California and Hawaii

To make sure we would have airliners flying directly over-head on this first leg, we would file our flight plans to fly west-bound, at low altitudes, five or six thousand feet, on high-altitude eastbound airways, the ones that the airlines would use. Several hours after departing the mainland, we would see the flashing strobes of the airliners flying overhead. We would contact them on the common emergency frequency, 121.5, and explain the situation to them; that we were ferrying airplanes to Hawaii, and could they give us a reading from their navigation instruments when they were directly overhead.

These conversations with the airline crews would usually go something like this…

"Traffic between waypoints Costs and Coppi on airway R-65, this is November 2068 Echo"

"Roger, 2068 Echo, this is United 732, go ahead."

"United 732, just wondering if you could help me out here. I'm at 5,000 feet on R-65, and would like a position fix from you, so I can check my navigation. I'll let you know when you are directly overhead. Over."

Long pause…

"Uhh, 2068 Echo, what kind of airplane are you flying?"

"A Cessna 182."

"And you're going where?"

"Going to Honolulu."

"Roger, 2068 Echo. How long of a flight is that?"

"Oh, about 17 hours."

"Geez! We're landing in San Francisco, going to the hotel downtown, seeing some sites and flying back to Hawaii tomorrow. We'll land before you do!"

On one such occasion, when we landed in Honolulu, there were two cases of cold beer, on ice, waiting for us from an airline crew we had spoken to earlier.

The second leg of our journey from Hawaii to American Samoa was the longest distance we would fly non-stop, 2600 miles and 17-19 hours of flight time. However, unlike the leg between California and Hawaii, if you ran into trouble, there were islands that you could divert to which were closer.

Those first few oceanic ferry flights I made were glorious. Most of the time we would fly as a group, but sometimes the planes were mismatched; one plane would be much slower than the others. In those cases, the slower plane, or planes, would takeoff first. A couple of hours later, the faster plane would take off on the same routing, and overtake us en route, landing ahead of us at our destinations. At least this way, we had someone to talk to during most of the crossing.

The day after getting back from my first ferry flight to Australia, I walked into the offices of Transair to turn in my expense report, receipts, and documentation for turning over the airplane to our customer. I was greeted by my fellow pilots and presented with a gift. There before me was the most beautiful, plastic portable urinal. This type of device was typically used by my male counterparts during long flights when 'nature called' and there was nowhere to land to use a bathroom. On the face of the container was a Transair decal, and on the wooden base shown a brass plaque which said,

HEIDI PORCH
FIRST OCEAN CROSSING
STARTED MARCH 9, 1982
COMPLETED MARCH 13, 1982

You're now one of "the boys"

I was hooked.

First Ocean Crossing award

Six

When You Gotta' Go…

And speaking of urinals, I am sure you are all saying to you self, 'But how do you go to the bathroom?' Okay, let's get this out of the way.

This was something I was quite concerned about prior to my first ocean crossing. I knew what the guys did. They just carried an empty plastic milk jug. No problem. But that wouldn't work for me. And I didn't know any other female ferry pilots that I could ask. I decided to do some research. The last thing I wanted to do was to wear an adult diaper! How humiliating.

I found a copy of a catalog dedicated to aviation products. In it was a device called a 'Jill's John.' How quaint. It comprised a plastic box with a carrying handle on top. Inside was an accordion-pleated plastic container. Protruding from the top was a long plastic tube. There was a separate elongated oval-shaped funnel that could be attached to the end of the tube. You can figure out the rest.

SUPER! Problem solved! Now I could relax and be able to enjoy a thermos of coffee, juice, and water. The 'hard' stuff would wait until we were on the ground. I was starting to worry that the device would not arrive in time, but the day of departure it arrived.

Sorry to get technical here, but it is important to understand the mechanics of the plane I was flying for you to appreciate the situation.

The model of aircraft I was flying for my first trip was a Cessna 206, also known as a Stationair. It was marketed as 'the sport-utility vehicle of the air,' popular among bush pilots. It would hold six passengers and had the option of a large cargo pod on the underside of the belly. On a side note, when I arrived at the airplane, a few hours before departure, I discovered that our mechanic, after removing all of the seats for tank installation, had replaced the pilot seat with a regular passenger seat. This particular seat did not have the controls to adjust the height of the seat. I had to improvise. I grabbed a smelly, old bathroom rug that had been in the back of my car, for who knows how long, folded it up, and used that to boost my sitting position in the seat. After flying in the heat for days, I smelled like a dirty, wet dog!

The 206 was powered by a Continental engine which required a specific plumbing installation for the ferry fuel system. Inside the cockpit were the usual forward and aft ferry tanks. Standard operating procedure was to take off and land using the wing tanks. Once in cruise, the pilot would switch off the wing tanks and start burning from the aft ferry tank. The fuel lines incorporated a 'vapor-return' feature, which meant that fuel being supplied to the engine was more than could be burned. This excess fuel would be returned through the vapor-return line and replenish the aft tank. Since the tank was being replenished, the engine could run off of the aft tank fuel for a very long time. Based upon the calculations of 'burn time,' the pilot would then switch to the forward ferry tank. The more experienced pilots would wait until the engine would actually show indications of fuel starvation before switching tanks, but I was not comfortable doing that, so I would just switch tanks when I calculated that the tank was close to being empty. After burning off the forward tank, you would then go back to the aft tank once again to burn that 'returned' fuel.

I had long finished my rather large thermos of coffee. And by this time, I had already switched from the aft tank to the forward tank. Finally, I realized that 'nature was calling.' Time to christen 'Jill's John'! Silly, but I looked around to see if my fellow pilots were anywhere close. I wriggled my pants down far enough to situate myself properly, and ... nothing.

Aft ferry tank, Cessna 206

No problem, I thought. Try again in a little while.

Twenty minutes later. Nothing. Without the feeling of cold porcelain on my behind, I had a mental block.

Well, maybe if I force fluids the 'dam' will burst. I took a few sips of water. I was sure that relief was just around the corner. Time to try again.

Nothing.

Now I was getting quite nervous. I could feel a dull ache in my lower back where my kidneys were. What was I going to do?

Try one more time.

Success! I experienced blessed relief. All of a sudden, the engine started surging and sputtering. I called out on the radio, "Bob, I've got a problem! Stand by!"

Instinctively, I immediately switched to the wing tanks and turned off the forward tank. It seemed like an eternity before the engine returned to its constant, steady hum. It was then that I realized that I had overlooked that the forward tank was going to burn much, much faster than the aft tank had. Even though I knew from my calculations about the time that the tank would run dry, in the back of my mind, I was still thinking that it would run longer than it had.

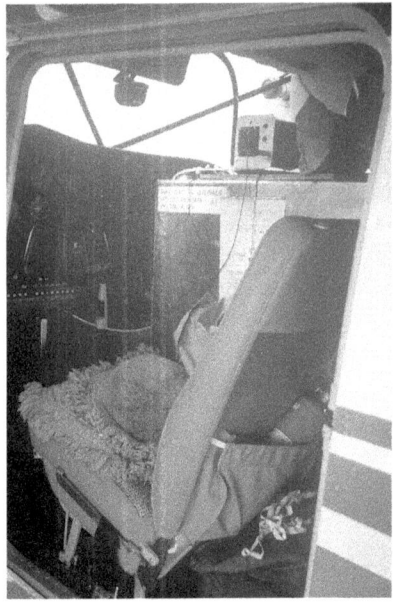

Forward tank with smelly rug on seat

Bob called. "You okay, Heidi?" I could sense the concern in his voice.

I replied, "You've heard the old adage, 'Getting caught with your pants down'?" And I explained to them what had happened.

After that experience, I never found the need to use 'Jill's John' again. There was no way I was going to go through *that* again! It wasn't the healthiest thing to do, but before each flight, I would have a cup of coffee, and by the time we got to the airport and finished pre-flighting, I would use the facilities to empty my bladder. During the flight I would ration my fluids. No more coffee. I would take occasional sips of water or fruit juice.

Glad we got that out of the way.

Seven

Solo

Eventually, it was time for me to make my first solo ocean crossing. I had mixed feelings about this. I absolutely loved being part of group, flying airplanes to exotic locales, taking in the local customs and culture, and enjoying the camaraderie of the other pilots. There were only about two dozen pilots in the world that ferried single-engine airplanes over the oceans professionally. I was proud to be one of them. But I knew that successfully completing a solo crossing would leave little to no doubt that I truly was 'One of the Boys.'

'The boys', Jay Prochnow, Jim York, Bob Grantham, Heidi

On several of the flights leading up to this, I had been given more responsibilities for the operation of the flight. I oversaw the filing of our flight plans, analyzed the wind trends over the preceding two weeks, and then took the lead in the navigation for the entire trip. They all felt that I was ready to go solo.

Fortunately, I was given a Cessna 210 for this trip. This was the fastest, and most comfortable of all the single-engine aircraft we ferried. AND it had an autopilot! This was real luxury. Most of the planes we flew had to be hand-flown.

I knew I was ready for this trip, but still, one could never anticipate every problem that could occur. Well, I found out about an hour into the trip. My LORAN didn't work. Should I turn back? I'd look like a 'wuss.' And besides, the LORAN only worked for part of the trip anyway. I would just have to 'dead reckon' the entire trip. Nothing I hadn't done before on other legs.

About halfway to Hawaii, I got a message over the HF radio from Honolulu Radio.

"Cessna 4911 Uniform, be advised… there has been a change to your route. Advise when you are ready to copy."

Damn.

"Go ahead, Honolulu," I answered while gripping my pencil with a shaky hand.

They proceeded to tell me that there were military war exercises being done in an area I wanted to traverse. They required that I cut south of my present course, join up with another airway, parallel my original route for 400 miles, then cut back north, join the original route, and continue to Honolulu.

Did I have enough fuel for this reroute? This had never happened to me before on any of the other ferry flights.

I got out my chart, plotted the new course, and calculated that I should land with about an hour's worth of reserve fuel. We normally would never depart on an overwater flight with less than a two to two-and-a-half hour fuel reserve. But I had no choice. There was nowhere to divert to that was any closer. And telling Honolulu Radio that I was unable to accept the new routing would probably require me to declare an emergency. I made a calculated decision to continue as instructed. Needless to say, my anxiety level increased with each passing minute.

I flew the newly assigned routing, and after several hours made the cut back northbound to the original airway. Where was I? Were my calculations accurate enough? Was I where I was supposed to be?

Thankfully, I saw a contrail coming up ahead of me.

"Traffic on R65 near CITTA intersection, you copy November 4911 Uniform?"

"November 4911 Uniform, this is American 401, go ahead."

"I'm a Cessna 210 on my way to Honolulu and was rerouted by ATC. My navigation radio is inop, and I was wondering if you could give me a position fix. I see a contrail coming up ahead of me and I'm wondering if it's you. Can you do an 'S' turn for me?"

"Sure thing!"

After several seconds, I could see that there was no curve, or break, in the contrail.

"American 401. I guess it's not you. Thanks anyway. Is there any other traffic on R65 near CITTA?"

"I think there is a Hawaiian Airlines flight behind us. Try them."

"4911 Uniform, this is Hawaiian 56. What do you need?"

I explained the situation to him and requested that he do an 'S' turn for me for identification. He complied, but the contrail stayed straight. By this time the original contrail was coming up quickly.

"Hey, 4911 Uniform. This is Pan Am 27. I think it might be us. Want us to do an 'S' turn for you?"

"Yes, please." I responded. I was really starting to get worried. Was I so far behind in my calculations that I was lost? Would I run out of fuel? By this time, in order for me to see the contrail, I had to do a 360-degree turn.

My heart sank. No break in the contrail.

"Thanks Pan Am, but it's not you."

I decided to point the plane towards the base of where the contrails originated from. That HAD to be in the vicinity of the Hawaiian Islands. I didn't care which island it was. It was land. I began to question my decision to accept the reroute. What would the others have done? Would this be my last trip with Transair? My imagination was getting the worst of me.

Just then, there was a crackle over the radio…

"Ahem…attention gentlemen. Never underestimate the power of a woman. All by herself, she has the entire sky doing 'S' turns!"

This announcement was followed by a series of microphone 'clicking,' and good-natured laughing. It was just what I needed to break the tension and get back to business.

As it turned out, I was exactly on course, but twenty to thirty miles closer than calculated. Catastrophe averted.

Upon landing in Honolulu, I refueled, filed my flight plan for the following day to Pago Pago, and filed a request for a weather briefing package. The worst was over. The rest of the flight should be a breeze. Since the LORAN reception petered out on the way to Samoa, I didn't see the need to take a delay for repairs.

Sometimes, we secretly wished for a mechanical or weather delay. Ferry flights operated under a section of Federal Aviation Regulations called 'Part 91.' Unlike the stricter regulations that the commercial airline crews flew under, Part 91 did not have any limits for the maximum number of hours a pilot could fly within a 24-hour period before a specified amount of rest was required. For instance, airline crews, flying internationally, are required by law to have four pilots on flights 12 hours, or longer. Half of that time is spent sleeping in a crew bunk so they would be fresh and alert for the landing. In talking on the radio to the occasional airline crew I was always envious when hearing about the hot meals they would be served, and the crew bunk they would retire to en route to get some shut-eye, not to mention having the use of a lavatory! The flying I was doing is what I referred to later in my career as 'paying my dues.'

The aircraft we delivered throughout the Pacific were insured against loss on an hourly basis. It was very expensive, and so there was always pressure to get the planes to their destinations as quickly as possible. Fatigue was always an issue, but it was just something that we all learned to deal with. Adrenaline was our 'friend.' It was difficult to just fall into bed after a long flight, sitting in one position for hours on end. Taking a walk, relaxing over a meal and a glass of wine helped to 'wind down.' Fortunately, the most tiring legs came at the beginning of a trip, with the last two legs after American Samoa much shorter and faster.

The flight to Pago Pago, American Samoa, was flight planned for 14 hours; a cakewalk when compared to some of the slower airplanes, which took around 18 hours. But even so, I was still using dead reckoning the entire way, with no landmarks in which to overfly.

The airport at Pago Pago did have a navigation beacon; a VOR radio, but the airport was in a lagoon on the far side of a mountain range that ran the length of the island. You had to be pretty much on top of the island before picking up a strong navigational signal. However, the airport controllers did have, what is known as DF or Direction-Finding capability. All they needed was for me to make a slow count over the radio, and they could give me a bearing to the airport.

So, after a 14-hour flight, nearly 2600 miles of open water, and using dead reckoning, I was told that I was 17 nautical miles west of track for the airport. Hallelujah! Time to celebrate!

There was only one decent hotel in Pago Pago; the Rainmaker Hotel. They had a main two-story structure, and several small island cottages. In its day, it was one of the more exclusive hotels in the Pacific. We stayed there often enough that the staff knew us by sight, and there was never a problem getting a room. But this time was different.

Rainmaker Hotel cottage

I walked up to the front desk, exchanged pleasantries with the desk clerk and asked for a room. I should have known something was off when I entered the lobby. The usually quiet space was full of people. On closer inspection, I noticed that they were all men…young men.

"I'm sorry Miss Porch, but we are full up."

"What? Nothing?"

"I'm afraid so, yes. You see, this morning an Australian submarine arrived, and the officers and crew will be staying here for several days."

The look of shock and panic on my face must have initiated a spark of sympathy for me because he then said, "But, let me see what I can do. I'll go talk to the manager. Wait here."

As I waited and said a silent prayer to the 'hotel Gods,' I noticed that I was getting a lot of stares. Pago Pago wasn't exactly a location where you saw very many single women hanging about. The guests were usually vacation couples, or businessmen, with the occasional Ham Radio aficionados that would travel to exotic locations to expand their repertoire of radio transmission locales.

Finally, the desk clerk returned with good news. He was

able to find me a room on the second floor. I could have kissed him! He gave me my key; I picked up my overnight bag and headed for the stairs. I no longer had to worry about sleeping in the airplane that night.

The next thing I knew, my bag was being taken from me by a man in his twenties, and uneasy on his feet. On the other side of me, my arm was being held by another twenty-something year old man, just as unsteady.

"We can't let a young lady walk to her room unescorted! Let us help you!" was said in a charming, but slurred, Aussie accent.

I tried to assure them that I was perfectly fine finding my room on my own, but they wouldn't hear of it. I reached my room door, and before I could get my bag back from them, they made me promise that I would meet them for a drink later. Two thoughts came to mind. One...I had been thinking of enjoying and relaxing over a drink for the past 2600 miles. And two... these guys were already 'three sheets to the wind,' and probably wouldn't remember asking me to join them anyway. I reluctantly accepted their invitation and said I would meet them in an hour. It was the only way I could get rid of them.

As tired as I was, I really did want to celebrate my success at completing the first two legs of my trip and overcoming the challenges I faced. The next two legs to Sydney were going to be a breeze, only a ten-hour flight to Norfolk Island, and a short six hours to Australia.

I found my 'second wind' and cleaned up to find myself walking into the lobby bar an hour later. It looked like something out of a movie; wall to wall men. And it seemed that they had been drinking since that morning. I was scanning the room for any place where I could find a secluded chair when a booming voice filled the room.

A large man in his 50's, obviously an American by the manner of his dress and his 'cowboy' accent, was standing up on one of the tables, and in a heavy Southern drawl shouted, "IF YA'LL SING 'THE EYES OF TEXAS ARE UPON YOU,' THE DRINKS ARE ON ME!"

Well, all hell broke loose. It didn't take me more than a few seconds to realize that I needed to get out of there…fast. Thankfully, I was able to slip out before I was recognized by my two 'escorts' from earlier.

I made my way over to the open-air restaurant and in short order was given a table for two by myself. Ahh. This was better. Now that well-deserved drink.

I was scanning the menu when I noticed a shadow creep over the top of the page. Oh good, the waiter is here. But, when I looked up, I saw a man in his thirties, nicely dressed in casual attire, and a beautiful smile on his face.

"Excuse me, miss." Ahh, another Aussie.

"My friends and I hate to see a beautiful woman eat alone. Would you care to join us?" as his head pointed to a nearby table where there were eight, equally handsome, gentlemen sitting, all looking my way.

"Are you from the sub that arrived this morning?"

"Yes, Miss. We are the officers."

My arm didn't need much twisting. Being called 'Miss' instead of 'Ma'am'… check. Cute Aussie accent… check. Eight gorgeous men… Double check.

Over the course of doing so many domestic ferry flights, by myself, I had gotten more comfortable being in situations where I had no company for meals. I was forced to get over the shyness I had experienced all my life. With Bob as my mentor, my confidence had grown in leaps and bounds, and I had gotten used to being around men most of the time. In fact, I was more comfortable being around men than I was with women.

I was wined and dined in fashion. They were fascinated by my 'story' of being a ferry pilot, and I with their life onboard a submarine. We stayed and watched the floor show of the performers doing traditional Polynesian dancing. The conversation flowed as well as the laughter.

As the evening was winding down, they asked me if I would like a tour of the sub. I have always had a fascination with the military and the war in the Pacific. My father had been in the Navy, and if women had been allowed to fly planes in the military at the time I finished high school, I would have enlisted for sure.

I didn't have to think about the invitation twice, and accepted immediately.

We took the short walk from the hotel down to the dock and I was given a tour. I gained a whole new appreciation of what they must go through living for weeks at a time in such cramped quarters.

We ended the tour in the officers 'mess,' which was just a small table in a booth setup. The captain explained to me a tradition of the Australian Navy. While at sea, the enlisted men are allowed the occasional glass of rum, while the officers drink Port. They presented me with a bottle of port wine. The label had a drawing of a boomerang and a kangaroo. The name of the wine was "Generating Red," which I learned was a slang term for battery acid. It also read, "Especially bottled for the Australian Submarine Squadron." They passed the bottle around, and each of the officers autographed the label for me. To this day, it is one of my most prized possessions.

Australian Submarine Squadron Port wine

The saying, 'An officer and a gentleman,' was never so true as it was during my evening with those men. They treated me with the utmost respect. I was escorted back to the hotel by two of my dinner companions, up to my hotel room door, all the while on the lookout to avoid the men that had 'helped' me to my room earlier. They each gave me a hug, and we exchanged farewells.

After takeoff the following morning, I did a brief detour and buzzed the submarine before taking up a heading for Norfolk Island. My 'wing rocking' was answered by several men waving back.

I was expecting the ten-hour flight to Norfolk Island to proceed without a hitch, but I was met by a line of thunderstorms a few hundred miles northeast of the island. Navigating around thunderstorms is difficult, at best, without the help of weather radar. Fortunately, most of the thunderstorms encountered over water, proved to be not as violent as over land, and especially at the lower altitudes. You just have to buckle in, stow loose objects, head for the lighter areas of the clouds, and hang on.

I broke out of the weather about 30 minutes later, but those 30 minutes felt like 30 hours. Norfolk Island appeared like a jewel against the brilliant blue of the water. Less tropical than most islands in the South Pacific, Norfolk Island is the home of 'Norfolk Island pine trees,' with thousands of them all over the island. They also boast of having the tallest fern trees on the planet.

This was my favorite fuel stop on the way to Australia. Norfolk has a fascinating history. The first European to have sighted Norfolk was Captain James Cook in 1774. But Norfolk is more commonly known for its history as being settled by mostly convicts, some of them transferred from Pitcairn Island, which were descendants from the HMS Bounty mutineers. Many of the islanders possess the last name of 'Christian,' as in Fletcher Christian.

The people there are warm and friendly, and I was always sorry to leave for the last leg to Sydney.

One final flight, and I could call my first oceanic solo a success.

Norfolk Island Airport

Norfolk Island coastline with pine trees

Sydney was only a six-hour flight from Norfolk. I could do it in my sleep. Fortunately, the weather was perfect, and I smiled as I passed by the Sydney Opera House off my left wing about to make my final approach into Bankstown Airport, about 17 miles west of the Sydney International Airport.

Sydney Harbor

I taxied up to the ramp outside the hangar where I was to turn over the keys. Where was the band? Where was the confetti? No banner that read, 'CONGRATULATIONS ON MAKING IT HERE ALIVE!' Nothing. Usually there would always be a few mechanics to greet us and tell us that they'd give us a ride to the nearest pub for a 'cold one.'

For whatever reason, the place was nearly deserted. I still had to remove all the radio equipment and ferry tank fittings used for plumbing the temporary fuel system for the ferry tanks. Looks like I would have to do it alone. What would normally take two hours, with some help, but alone it took me four. I managed to remove and pack up everything that belonged to Transair, take a shower in the hangar bathroom, all the while hoping that none of the workers would walk in on me, and get a lift over to Sydney International for the return flight on Pan Am that evening. No rest for the weary.

I learned a lot during those first few over-water trips. I learned about the anomalies of navigation and radio communications. I learned how to scrounge for engine oil at airports with no services. And I learned about hazardous weather flying techniques.

For my Pan Am flight home, I was missing Homer. He was usually the one that would get us upgraded to First Class, but I took a chance anyway by purchasing a couple of bottles of gin while I was in Pago Pago…just in case.

I approached the ticket agents at the Pan Am ticket counter, and before I could say anything, he cheerfully asked, "Where's Homer?"

"Here," I said, as I presented him with both bottles of gin. "Homer couldn't make it this trip, but he wanted you to have these."

Mission accomplished!

Eight

Rubberduck

If one is lucky enough, a person comes into your life that inspires you, encourages you, supports you, and makes you a better person. For me, that was Bob.

I had grown up an extremely shy person. I would be the child that would hang onto my mother's skirt, my face hidden, whenever meeting strange people. Of course, I was comfortable, and quite the 'ham,' at holiday family reunions and neighborhood parties, but I think I was in junior high school before I ever went by myself into a store to buy something. I still avoid confrontations of any kind. And even though I had a steely determination to accomplish my dream of becoming an airline pilot, I went through my flying journey with a certain lack of self-confidence. That is… until Bob.

Those early days flying for Transair allowed me to spend a lot of time with Bob, and another ferry pilot, Jim York. The three of us were usually always together, if not on a group domestic ferry flight, then getting together for a few beers, or just hanging out at the airport or glider port, where I still occasionally did some towing.

After that first flight with the Transair gang, from Vacaville to Wichita, Bob took me under his wing, so to speak, and attempted to teach me the finer points of what it takes to become a good ferry pilot. Whenever we would bring back a couple of planes from the factory, he was always imparting his knowledge of emergency planning, weather considerations, aircraft performance, and navigation. It was a Masters course in Ferry Flying 101.

But it wasn't until I started flying over water that I truly appreciated Bob's expertise and guidance. Learning to navigate over long expanses of open water was nothing you could gain from books. Most of the time it was just a 'feeling' that you had as to whether you needed a course correction, or not. How much trust did you place in your weather briefing? And then, once the decision was made to make a correction, did you apply one degree? Five degrees? Ten? And for how long? And how precisely could you hold that revised heading? You're dog-tired and there was usually no autopilot to rely upon for accuracy. These things had to be taught in the moment.

Over the course of those early ocean flights, Bob shared all this knowledge. He never told me when I had made a wrong decision. Rather, he would ask me the reasons why I had made a particular decision, and through those questions, I would discover on my own where I had made an error in calculation or judgment. His instruction was always offered in good humor and encouragement. He was plentiful in his praise when I had done a good job. Ever so slowly, I found my confidence increasing with each flight.

On my third oceanic ferry flight to Australia, we were nearly halfway to Pago Pago. The three of us were flying as a group, Bob, Jim, and myself. We had hit that 'lull' during the flight when we had run out of things to say, we didn't feel like breaking up the monotony by flying tight formation, we were on course, and just cruising along. All was quiet. Then, I was startled by an ungodly noise coming over the speakers. It sounded like someone was jumping up and down on a set of bagpipes. Turns out it was a kazoo! And then I could make out the tune, if you could call it that, of the sort of song you'd hear at a military parade. It went on for about 30 seconds, and then I heard Bob yelling over the radio,
"CONGRATULATIONS, HEIDI! YOU JUST
BROKE ONE THOUSAND HOURS!"

How did he know that? Jim added his words of congratulations. Bob had somehow been keeping track of my flight hours. He must have taken a peek at my logbook at some point, and then kept track of all of my subsequent flights until he knew the precise moment when I broke that all important 1000-hour mark. I'll never forget it.

On the last leg of that trip, going into Sydney, Bob, Jim, and I were discussing upcoming flights and decisions that needed to be made regarding logistics, etc. I don't recall the exact topic we were discussing, but I clearly remember Bob saying, "Well, Heidi, when you truly become a ferry pilot, you'll understand."

I felt a wave of indignity wash over me, and before I knew it, I picked up the mike, and said, "What do you mean? I *AM A FERRY PILOT!*"

I heard Bob chuckle, and say, "That's what I've been waiting to hear." His voice was full of pride. I knew then that he had been goading me into realizing my self-worth. It was a wonderful gift.

We became the best of friends. He was my mentor, my 'cheerleader,' my 'rock' when I needed support. So, it came as no surprise when those feelings turned into love.

Bob was older than me; about 18 years. He had enlisted in the Air Force at just 17 years old. And while his dream was to be an Air Force pilot, he was not able to pass the physical, and so he spent his military years as a Loadmaster for cargo planes, but he flew during his off-duty time. Early in his enlistment he was sent overseas to Japan. There he met a local girl, they got married and had two children. When he left the military, re-enlisting several times, he went straight into ferry flying. It was what he loved most. He had no other aspirations of flying corporately or commercially. Maybe that's why he was so good at what he did.

The fact that there was an age difference did not matter. Bob was one of the 'youngest' persons I had ever known. He was full of life and always drew the attention of those around him. He was admired and respected throughout the ferry flying community.

And at nearly every airport we flew to in the Pacific, everyone knew Rubberduck.

Needless to say, I struggled with the fact that I had fallen in love with someone who was married. I felt ashamed and worried about hurting his wife and children. I didn't want people thinking the worst of me. I used to discuss this with Jim when I needed a sounding board. He explained to me that Bob, and his wife, were basically living separate lives, and had been for a long time. That didn't help. The guilt I felt was tortuous. It was a constant cloud hanging over my head. I used to think, wouldn't it be wonderful if we knew the exact moment when fondness turns to love, and we could just 'turn back' before the moment strikes, before having to deal with the consequences? But love doesn't work like that. It sneaks up on you until it's too late.

Bob had always been a considerate and sentimental man, not afraid to express his feelings. Sometimes this would make me feel uncomfortable because I was always trying to make our relationship appear to others as one that was only professional and friendly. The only person that knew the truth about our feelings was Jim. My parents and siblings did not know, even though Bob had become an unofficial member of the family. My father would 'talk shop' with Bob about airplanes and flying, and my mother loved his easy-going manner. Bob was always teasing my mother good-naturedly, and she got a kick out of the attention. Part of me thought that our connection was something that would endure as a special closeness for the rest of our lives, but I doubted that it would ever turn into something permanent.

Marriage was not on my radar. My focus was on having a career with the airlines. Back in the early 80's, the airlines were barely hiring, and age 30 was the kiss of death. Your chances of getting hired if you were older than 30 were just about nil. I knew that I had to give all my attention to getting as much flying time as I could, and to bombard every airline I could think of with my resumé and applications. If there was a job offer, you couldn't be picky. You took whatever job offer you got because seniority was everything. The date you were hired and the seniority that grew from it dictated where you would be based, what aircraft you would fly, how soon you could upgrade to First Officer, Captain, or remain as a Flight Engineer, or Second Officer. Seniority was everything. With such uncertainty of where I would end up, how could I seriously consider committing to a serious relationship? I knew that Bob did not care. He would have supported any decision I made when it came to my career. I believe that he would have followed me wherever I ended up, making whatever accommodations he needed to with his work.

I didn't realize just how serious Bob was until one evening at dinner, when he gave me a stunning ring with seven blue sapphires and five diamonds. I had seen it at an art gallery in Sydney on an earlier trip. Bob noticed and went back to buy it but held onto it for months waiting for the right time to give it to me. And as much as I loved the sentiment behind the gesture, it also added to my inner turmoil of how to deal with the situation.

It was during this time that I was being prepared for my first oceanic solo crossing. Transair had experienced a busy surge in deliveries to Australia and New Zealand. We had five crossings in a seven-week period. For the last two ferries, I had been given most of the responsibilities. They were grooming me to be on my own. I was physically and emotionally exhausted. There were times when I would wake up in a hotel room on some Pacific Island and have to look at the phone book to see where I was.

On the last ferry trip of this surge, it was Bob, our boss, Earl, and me. I knew that Earl would be scrutinizing my performance, and I was nervous because I was so tired. Bob and I had decided to have a discreet frequency to use so we could talk privately, should I have a question or concern come up during the trip.

When we landed in Honolulu, our first layover, while re-fueling I walked over to discuss something with Bob. When I started walking back to my airplane, I could see that Earl was standing by the open doorway to my cockpit. He was leaning inside, although I could not tell what he was looking at. Deciding he was just making sure everything looked in order, I didn't think any more about it.

The next day was our long leg to Pago Pago. The flight was going normally, no problems. Bob and I continued to use our discreet frequency to discuss things, and as I feared, our talk turned to personal matters. We discussed our feelings for one another, my doubts, and concerns. I tried to explain that all of my efforts had to go towards my career. I wasn't sure that I could handle a relationship. There were moments when my emotions got the best of me, and I cried. And there were times when, and I'm not proud of this, we voiced our objections to some of Earl's decisions regarding how the flight operation was run. That afternoon, after landing in Pago Pago, we dicussed what time we would all meet for dinner. Earl told us that he would not be joining us, and to go without him. Odd. We always ate together. Maybe he just wanted to sleep.

Upon arriving in Sydney (Bankstown), we got to work packing up for our return flight to the States. Earl remained aloof. When we arrived in San Francisco, Earl said, "I want to see both of you in my office tomorrow morning at 9:00."

What? Huh? We had just spent the last five days together. What did he need to talk to us about?

That next morning, Bob and I found ourselves sitting opposite Earl and Bruce, the other partner of Transair, in Bruce's office.

Earl looked at us sternly and said, "It has become known to me that the two of you are having a romantic relationship."

I wanted to die. I was praying that the floor would open up and bury me. I was speechless. Bob could see my discomfort and challenged Earl. Frankly, I don't even remember what he said as I was in shock. All I know is that the next thing I remember is Earl slamming his hand down on the desk and saying, "Does the frequency 123.55 mean anything to YOU?"

And then it hit me. While in Honolulu, Earl had suspected that Bob and I had been talking on a private frequency. He went over to my cockpit, powered on the battery, and found the frequency that was dialed into my VHF radio. He had been listening in on our conversations for days. My brain immediately tried to recall every conversation we had shared during those days. I'm sure that we had said things that hurt Earl's feelings and wounded his ego.

I floated back to the current conversation, and there was a discussion going on about having us fired. I could tell from the look on Bob's face that he was ready to tell Earl what he could do with his job, or something to that effect, but then Bob would look at me, see my tears, my humiliation, and he knew that I needed to keep this job. I needed the flight hours. Bruce, I could tell, was wishing he could be anywhere else but where he was. He seemed as uncomfortable with what was going on as I was.

It was decided that we could stay on, and even though it took every ounce of self-control on Bob's part, we both apologized for our comments about Earl, and frankly, I don't remember anything else about the rest of the meeting. I was in a haze of self-reproach, embarrassment, and anger.

I left the meeting feeling devastated and humiliated. I wanted to be alone. This whole ordeal had pushed me over the edge. If I had had any doubts of whether to continue my relationship with Bob, or resort to just being friends, this had made things clearer. Bob could sense from my manner that something had changed, but he gave me the space I needed and did not push.

Over the next few weeks, life at work eventually went back to a feeling of normalcy. I even flew a trip as Bob's co-pilot delivering a Beechcraft Queenair to Japan. But by that time, I had decided that I couldn't handle the guilt I was feeling and the uncertainty of what the future would hold. I started to put more distance between me and Bob. I knew that Bob was hurt at my 'coolness,' but we were still able to be professional. Maybe it was because we started off as friends.

We continued working together on trips and saw each other socially, from time to time. Bob was patient and understanding of my feelings. And over the following seven to eight months, I discovered that being able to 'stand back' from our relationship gave me the time I needed to appreciate all over again the wonderful qualities of this man. Time has a way of bringing clarity to the heart. Perhaps, one day, we could work something out.

It was now December, and Bob and I had plans to have dinner upon his return from his next ferry flight to New Zealand. I was planning on telling him that I was ready to think about planning for our future. It would be my Christmas gift to him.

Bob and Homer

Nine

Early morning. The phone rang. I answered.

"Oh, Heidi. Thank God you're there." It was Bruce calling from his office.

"Why? What's happened?"

"Bob went down last night. He was delivering a twin-engine plane to New Zealand for Brents Aviation, and one of the engines quit. The last radio call that Honolulu received was that he was at 500 feet and wasn't able to maintain altitude. This morning, the Coast Guard found some debris floating in the area of his last known position. He had a passenger with him, and I was afraid it might have been you."

Knowing Bob as I did, I knew that he would have tried to get into 'ground effect' to extend his range, but something inside of me told me that he was gone.

Bob was one of the most experienced and talented pilots I had ever known. He had drilled it into me on nearly every flight we had flown together that you get your ELT turned on as soon as you realize that you have to ditch. An ELT, Emergency Locator Transmitter, is a device that when sensing an impact exceeding a certain threshold automatically emits an emergency signal on 121.5 that can be located by rescue ships and aircraft. That is why commercial aircraft are required to monitor this frequency on their secondary communication radios. There had been no signal which told me that Bob did not know just how close he was to going into the water.

It had been a moonless night. On nights like that we sometimes had to tape our navigational charts in front of the windshield so we couldn't see outside, because the stars were so bright, and with no moon you could not see the surface of the ocean. It would induce extreme vertigo where you would swear that you were in a descending turn, when in actuality, your wings were straight and level. The only way Bob would have been able to see the surface of the water would be to turn on his landing lights. The landing lights were attached to the landing gear. For him to turn on the lights to see the surface of the water, he would have had to lower the gear. No longer would he have a smooth undersurface in which to 'ride' the ground effect. He would have been trying to get into the buffer of air, just a few feet above the surface of the water, a 'cushion' of sorts, where a plane which was technically too heavy to fly, could 'float' along on this buffer of air. If Bob had realized just how close he was, he would have turned on the ELT that he wore on his survival vest. He would not have trusted that the force of the impact would trigger the ELT to start transmitting.

I experienced a mix of emotions. I felt grief, guilt, and remorse. I wouldn't have the chance to tell him that there might be a way back to one another. I was angry. Why him? He was so experienced. Strangely, I also felt a sense of peace that he went the way he would have wanted. He would have continued doing ferry flying for the rest of his life.

Two days after Bob's memorial service, I was flying in what would have been Bob's 100th airplane across the ocean. Unbeknownst to me, months earlier, Bob had told the owner of Brents Aviation, the other outfit that we did ferry flights for on occasion, that if anything ever happened to him, that I would have 'debs' on those flights. I knew how important that 100th airplane was to Bob. Bob had been looking forward to joining the International Ferry Pilots Club. You had to make 100 oceanic ferry deliveries in order to qualify. His friends in New Zealand were planning a huge celebration party for him. Bob had loaded up the plane (this one was a twin-engine, so it had extra room for cargo) with gifts for everyone, a bicycle for the son of his friend, a yellow garden hose for his friend's wife, and other items. The search and rescue planes found the yellow garden hose floating near the crash site.

I got through that flight in an emotional haze. My parents did not want me to go. But the thought of any other person touching that airplane was unacceptable. I had to do it. Bob would have wanted it that way. I was paired up with another airplane. The pilot would be Dave who was a Naval Aviator out of Alameda Naval Air Station. He had a limited amount of time to do this flight, as he had a full-time commitment to the Navy. I had not slept much leading up to Bob's memorial, and the night before the flight. I would have preferred to delay the trip a few days, but Dave's schedule was tight. I knew Dave, but not well. He was aware that this would be a difficult trip for me and was understanding.

Bob's 100th airplane, New Zealand

On that first leg from Oakland to Hawaii, I had brought some flowers from the memorial service to drop at the crash site. I was descending to get a little bit closer to the surface and asked Dave if he had ever dropped anything out of an airplane before. I wasn't sure what would be the best airspeed. We were discussing this on the common frequency, which happened to be 121.5, the emergency frequency that all airliners are required to monitor during oceanic flights. We should have been on our own discreet frequency. I was telling Dave that I was descending down to around one thousand feet before opening the window.

"Hey, aircraft descending down to 1,000 feet. Do you need assistance? This is United 548."

"No, thank you."

Dave proceeded to tell him what had happened to Bob.

I was too emotional to add to the conversation. How could I sum up what Bob had meant to me in a few words to a bunch of strangers? And I wanted to keep it private.

Bob at Rainmaker Hotel

As I opened the window and dropped the flowers, realizing that it would be the closest I would ever be to him again, there was a brief moment when I considered continuing the descent to the water. Part of me wanted to be with him. Not one second after that thought came into my head, I could imagine Bob saying,

"Oh no you don't! You've got too much to live for. Get your butt back up into the sky!"

Just then, I heard numerous airliners call out on the radio,

"God speed, Bob"

"God Bless, Bob"

"Peace be with you, Bob"

How I love pilots.

Ten

3 AM August 12, 1984
Cessna 182, N8032M

I could never sleep the night before a ferry trip, and tonight was no exception. Typically, we would launch on our first leg to Hawaii anywhere between 1:00 and 3:00 AM, in order to arrive in Hawaii early afternoon. That would give us time to refuel, submit a request for a thorough weather briefing packet from the National Weather Service, and to file a flight plan for the next leg of our journey. I would try to get a few hours of sleep beforehand, but being a light sleeper, it was difficult. What made it more challenging on this particular trip was that we had family friends staying with us from out of town. I was living with my parents at that time, the condo I had been renting had been sold, so it was a temporary arrangement as my parents' house was extremely small. And as hard as my mother tried to keep the noise down, it just wasn't possible.

I always disliked the few hours before a trip. I can't say that I was nervous or apprehensive. It was more of a tenseness that I really could not explain. I needed to be focused. It was no time for idle chitchat with those nearby. There were things to do.

Even though in the preceding days I had studied the trends in the winds for the crossing, I still needed to do a final check of the weather forecast for the route. Based upon the current winds, I had to plot my course and calculate the estimated time en route for each of the 15 waypoints along the route, as well as the fuel consumption. We would never take off for a flight unless we had a minimum of two, to two and a half hours of reserve fuel.

N8032M the morning of departure, Nut Tree Airport

Forward ferry tank, LORAN and HF radios

Typically, the afternoon before the flight, a final runup of the engine would be done, as well as a compass check. The magnetic compass could be off by several degrees based not only upon the magnetic variation between true and magnetic North, which varies around the earth, but also magnetic deviation, which is caused by the magnetic fields created by the aircraft's equipment on board. One degree of error carried for 60 miles, and you would be off course by one mile. Multiply that for over thousands of miles, and on the leg between Hawaii and Pago Pago, you could be off course by over 40 miles. The island is only 18 miles long, so you could easily miss land altogether. It was important to get this check done prior to any long-distance flights, along with a thorough preflight inspection of the aircraft. Finally, you had to find space in the cramped confines of the cockpit for packing the rest of your gear; life raft, flight bag, survival equipment and suitcase. In order to install the two aluminum ferry tanks, the co-pilot's seat and the passenger seats had to be removed. They were broken down, placed in large garbage bags, and stowed in the tail compartment. Fortunately, the FAA had allowed us to be up to 30% over the aircraft's certified gross weight in order to make these flights. The very last task I would accomplish would be to tape a photo of Bob on the gas tank to my right.

Aft ferry tank

As was our custom, my parents would usually drive me out to the airport before departing on an overwater flight. But this time, our family friends, and my sister, Allison, accompanied them, as well. While I would have preferred to be by myself, I understood their need to spend time with me. I always had the feeling that they weren't too keen about my ferry flying. I would always call them after I arrived in Honolulu on the first leg of any delivery flight, and no matter what time it was, they would always answer my call on the first ring, like they were sitting by the phone until they heard from me.

I had a feeling of anxiety at the prospect of having to 'entertain' them while I was trying to concentrate on what had to be done. It was a distraction. I didn't feel like explaining what I was doing, and what all the equipment was for, etc. Along with that, I was paired up with my boss, Earl. I didn't know how he would feel about extra people milling about. I tried to be as cheerful as possible, but I'm sure I wasn't doing a very good job of it.

With my preflight preparation complete, and going over any last-minute logistics with Earl, I said my 'good-byes' to my family, and climbed into the cockpit. The airport, at that time of night, hours before sunrise, was always calm and peaceful. I always felt a bit guilty turning over the engine and disrupting the serenity by the noise of the airplane's engine coming to life. I was just about to release the brakes to start my taxi when I heard a knock on the window to my left. There was my mother, motioning me to open the door. What the hell! Didn't she realize that she was in danger being so close to the nearly invisible spinning propeller? I cracked open the window, and my mother was yelling at me over the blast of the propwash.

"DO YOU HAVE YOUR RAFT?"

Again, I thought, *What the hell!*

Of course, I have my life raft! I thought. If I didn't pack anything else, I would have my raft!

Looking back on that moment, I should have known that my mother's sixth-sense had flared up. In 1968, our father had accepted a new job which required us to relocate from our home in Hayward, California, to Long Island, New York. He had gone ahead of us in order to start his new job, and to find a house for us to live in. The rest of us, my mother, two sisters and I, stayed behind to sell our house and pack our belongings. It was decided that we three girls would join our father a few months later, and our mother would stay behind to tie up loose ends. We had our airline tickets purchased for our upcoming flight back east for Jan. 31, 1969, and all other arrangements had been made. But the day before our departure my mother announced that she had changed her mind. We would go the following week. No reason was given. I'm sure this caused some consternation with my father as he had already made plans to leave work for the drive to Kennedy Airport to pick us up.

The next day, we were watching the evening news when the lead story was announced. A DC-8 airliner had been hijacked from San Francisco to Cuba. That was the same flight we would have been on. Maybe my mother's 'little voice' was trying to tell her something again when she felt that she had to make sure that I had my raft.

Earl was flying a slightly slower airplane, a Cessna 172, which meant that I would be throttled back a bit so we could stay together. I wasn't too concerned about not flying at a higher power setting, as this particular airplane was not new from the factory. It was from a previous owner, so the engine had been 'seasoned.' At 120 to 125 KIAS (knots indicated airspeed) or 138 to 143 miles per hour, it would take us 17 hours and 53 minutes to fly from California to Honolulu, Hawaii. Our ultimate destination was Christchurch, New Zealand, on the South Island. It would take us four days to get there.

As soon as we were airborne, that tenseness I had felt in the preceding hours evaporated. I was 'home' again. There was something about seeing the abrupt edge of the city lights along the coast near San Francisco, and the expanse of blackness beyond that was magical.

Just before sunrise, we could see the flashing strobe lights of airliners overhead on their way back to California from Hawaii. As was the custom, we contacted one of them and got a position fix to compare against our own calculations. We were on track and on time.

Sometimes, to break the monotony of the long hours, we might fly in formation for 20 to 30 minutes. The first time I did this, which was on my first ocean crossing, I was initiated to formation flying by the strange sight of, what we called, 'Pressed Ham.' One of the pilots would pull his pants down and press his bare buttocks against the window for all to see. But not today.

There were no cell phones in which to stream music back then, so I brought along tape cassettes of some of my favorite musicians, Billy Joel, the Beatles, Doobie Brothers, Elton John, Kenny Loggins. Usually, at some point along the trip you would trade music with your partners, just for a change of pace. But most of the time, I just enjoyed the beauty of my surroundings. I appreciated how the scenery would change every hour. I just wish it had been quieter. We all wore David Clark headsets, which in those days were quite heavy, hot, and cumbersome. No such thing as noise-cancelling headsets then.

Another habit I had gotten into, to break the monotony, was to perform a 'ditching drill' every couple of hours. I would make believe that the engine had just quit, and I went through a mental checklist, of sorts, which I would time. This would entail making a fake radio call declaring an emergency, plotting my position on the chart, and donning my life vest. After doing several of these 'dry runs,' I would easily shave a couple of minutes off of my time by the end of the flight.

We settled in and I looked forward to enjoying some fresh Hawaiian pineapple that evening.

Eleven

"Earl, I think I have a problem."

It was about eleven hours into our 18-hour flight. At each checkpoint, a crosscheck was made of the flight's progress; a kind of 'How Goes It,' where we would record the actual time over a point, the estimated time for the next waypoint, the planned heading vs. the actual heading, true airspeed, ground speed, fuel consumption and a monitor of the engine readings. This was usually the point where a position report would be made over the HF radio to ARINC, Aeronautical Radio Incorporated. The controlling ARINC sector would forward the position report to Air Traffic Control.

Everything looked fairly normal, although I noticed that the oil pressure, which was usually at the top of the 'green,' or normal range arc, at 60 psi, was about five psi low. This was normal on most flights. The outside air temperature grew warmer as we flew south into Pacific waters, and since the engine would be running for such a long duration, it was typical that the oil viscosity would thin out, causing a slight drop in the pressure. The oil temperature remained steady at 30% of the green arc.

About 20 minutes later, I looked at the oil pressure gauge again during my normal scan, and noted that the oil pressure had dropped another 5 psi. This was not normal. It was now down to around 50 psi. A sick feeling fluttered in my stomach.

"Earl...I think I have a problem."

I explained to him the situation, and asked him if he would take a closer look at the belly of my plane and around the engine area, to see if there were any signs of smoke or an oil leak. He eased his way over and did a thorough inspection of my plane.

"I don't see anything abnormal, Heidi."

Crap. Was the engine just using too much oil? Was I making a mountain out of a molehill? Maybe it would settle down and stabilize. But my gut was telling me that something was wrong.

"What do you wanna do, Heidi?"

I thought, 'Is this where I call a Mayday? A real honest-to-God MAYDAY? That only happens in the movies, right?' But this was real, not make-believe. Maybe it was just an instrumentation problem, and I'd call a Mayday for nothing. But then again...what if it gets worse, and I wait too long to call for help? We were still almost seven hours from land.

I paused before answering, considering all of the ramifications. With resignation in my voice, I replied, "I think I better call for help, Earl."

"Are you sure?"

This caught me off guard. Earl should have known me well enough by now, with all of the flying we had done together, that I would never consider a decision like that lightly.

I forced through the lump in my throat and responded, "Yup."

"Well … go ahead."

That curt response from Earl gave me the feeling that I was alone in this. That little tickle of uneasiness in my stomach was now full-blown fear.

I picked up the microphone for the HF Radio, took a few moments to collect my thoughts, and made the call.

"Honolulu Radio. November 8032 Mike on 8843."

I waited for what seemed an eternity for Honolulu to respond. Was this really happening?

"8032 Mike, this is Honolulu. Go ahead."

"Honolulu, 8032 Mike. I think I have a… *possible* Mayday."

A Navy P-3 Orion, also known as an anti-submarine surveillance aircraft, flying in my vicinity, heard my call over the radio. Bill Piersig, the Captain, commented to his crew, "*POSSIBLE* Mayday? You're either pregnant, or you're not!"

"Affirmative, Honolulu. I am slowly losing oil pressure, and I am not sure how long the engine will continue to run. I am declaring an emergency and requesting assistance."

That simple request put into motion a blur of activity, not only physically, but mentally and emotionally. Honolulu needed more information to pass on to the Coast Guard Search and Rescue Center; souls on board, current position, estimate for next position, fuel on board, the type of emergency and survival equipment I had. In their request for my position both Earl and I plotted our position based upon the LORAN readings we had. Unfortunately, we were in an area about halfway between the Oakland area of LORAN coverage, and the Honolulu area. It was fairly accurate in telling you if you were north or south of tract, but not very accurate as to how far along the route you were. At the same time, Earl and I were still trying to troubleshoot the problem. Maybe I overlooked something. The engine was running smoothly, but the oil pressure was still dropping ever so slowly. It was now at 45 psi.

Those first few minutes after the call to Honolulu felt chaotic in my mind. It was hard to keep my thoughts straight. I felt as though I should be doing a hundred things at once, and I couldn't help but feel as though I was forgetting to do things. I kept getting calls from Honolulu, from Earl and from well-meaning aircraft listening in on the emergency frequency. This was going to drive me crazy unless I did something. A mantra kept running through my head; 'Is this really going to happen?'

The uncertainty of the situation finally forced me to say to myself, 'Heidi, make up your mind! You are either going to be able to nurse this airplane on to Hawaii, or you are going to 'get wet.' Which is it?'

Right then, somehow, I knew that it was going to be the latter. And then, it was as though a switch had been thrown. My mind immediately calmed down, and it was almost as if I was watching myself from another vantage point; a sort of out-of-body experience.

Once I had finished giving all of the requested information to Honolulu ARINC, a different call came over the VHF radio.

"8032 Mike, this is Papa Quebec 857. We are a P-3 based out of Moffett Field. Did you just give a position report for estimating Citta intersection about 20 minutes ago?"

"Yes, I did."

"And can you confirm what kind of airplane are you in?"

"A Cessna 182."

"Hell!" Captain Bill Piersig said to his crew. "That is a BONA FIDE Mayday!"

"Well, I think we just passed you. We are headed for San Francisco from Hawaii on the same airway. You want us to turn around and see if we can intercept you?"

"That would be much appreciated!" I said in my professional pilot voice. But my mind was screaming, "HELL, YES!" I mean, it was one thing to have your wingman by your side, but to have a Navy airplane nearby with better communications and the ability to help coordinate rescue vessels to help with the search was more than I could ask for. I passed along the closest estimate I had for my position, but it was rough, certainly not accurate enough for locating such a tiny target.

Earl noticed a couple of contrails coming up in front of us. After a few radio calls, they were identified as belonging to two 747s, United and Qantas. They had been listening in on the common emergency frequency, 121.5, which was what the P-3 and I had been using, and they knew of my situation. I asked the Qantas crew to do an 'S' turn, and sure enough, they were the second contrail. When they were directly overhead, they were able to give me a much more precise latitude and longitude from their onboard INS, Inertial Reference System. I needed to take a break from all of the inquiries I had been receiving, and so I asked Earl to plot the coordinates the Qantas crew had given me. It showed that we were on track. I passed the coordinates on to the P-3 crew. Without these more precise coordinates, it was doubtful that anyone would have been able to find me. But now I felt more confident that help was on the way.

During this time, I had decided that I should give myself a little more 'breathing' room for when, and if, the engine quit. We had been flying at around six thousand feet, but I started a slow 100 foot per minute climb up to 8,500 feet, which would give me some extra time in a descent. I decided to reduce the power a bit on the engine to reduce the load. This was totally contrary to my instinct to go 'balls to the wall' and fly as fast as I could to get to land. But, maybe by powering back, it would help the engine run longer. I also took a few minutes to don my life vest. This wasn't one of those fake 'drills' I had practiced during previous flights. This was now the real thing.

Captain Piersig, Bill, continued chatting with me about the survival equipment I had on board, as well as personal topics, like why was I doing this sort of flying, how long had I been doing it, where did I live, etc. It made me wonder if he was the sort of guy that liked listening to himself talk, or if he was just, by nature, a chatty fellow. I didn't mind. It kept my mind occupied, distracting me from the seriousness of the situation. I didn't realize at the time that there was a purpose in his interest. He was trying to assess my mental state to see how I would handle things once the shit hit the fan. But our conversations had the added effect of giving me a sense of comfort. It did not take long for me to surmise that Captain Piersig and his crew cared about my well-being. It helped me to relax and think clearly.

While waiting for the P-3 to locate me, Earl asked, "Heidi, do you want to have Honolulu Radio make a call to your folks to let them know what's going on?"

"No! We still have over six hours of flying before we get to Hawaii. Maybe it *is* just an instrumentation problem. Even though the pressure is still dropping, the oil temperature is normal, as is everything else. I don't want them worrying all that time. Wait until we know for sure."

The thought of alarming my family with the possibility that I was in danger was abhorrent to me. There would be time enough for that in the coming hours.

The needle on the oil pressure gauge was now hovering just above the red line; zero.

About 15 minutes later, an hour and a half since I had called the Mayday, I heard those blessed words come over the radio.

"32 Mike, this is Papa Quebec 857. We have you in sight."

Twelve

The Strategy

The P-3 was at 28,000 feet when they answered my call. They descended down to 15,000. This was a much better altitude to keep me in sight without burning too much fuel. They contacted the Coast Guard Search and Rescue, SAR, Coordination Center at Barbers Point, Hawaii, to inform them of the P-3's involvement in my rescue and to find out when, and if, an Alert plane would be dispatched to my location. The P-3 was advised that they were going to dispatch a C-130 that was currently airborne on another 'distress' mission west of Oahu.

Now that the P-3 was 'on station,' Capt. Piersig suggested that I attempt to contact him on the portable ELT I carried in the bag of survival equipment that was kept directly behind my seat. This was different from the one that was mounted in the aft fuselage. This transceiver could transmit a locator signal manually on both 121.5 and the military frequency of 243 MHz. But more importantly, it had a voice function. I extended the antenna out the left window, and transmitted, hoping that the P-3 would be able to pick up my transmission and signal. This proved futile. They were not able to pick up any voice transmission or signal. This was a depressing turn of events. I was counting on having a working transceiver to have with me in the raft to be able to communicate with the rescue airplanes.

The crew of the P-3 suggested that I take up a heading of 242 degrees and divert to Hilo, which was about a hundred miles closer than Honolulu. And from their vantage point, at the higher altitude, the P-3 crew could assess the direction and strength of the swells much better than I could at my altitude. Should I have to ditch, they suggested a heading of 260 degrees to touch down parallel with the swells. Fortunately, the winds appeared to be light, five to ten knots. It was also suggested that I 'stall' the airplane in. This would ensure that I would be flying at the slowest possible airspeed prior to touching down. When an airplane 'stalls,' the airflow over the wing is interrupted, thereby providing no 'lift.' With no airflow over the control surfaces, moving the control yoke has no effect. The wing is no longer flying, and the pilot has no control.

This maneuver concerned me. It wasn't like I was going to land on a flat surface, where I knew exactly when touchdown would occur. The landing surface was constantly oscillating up and down. If I stalled the airplane the least bit too high, and one wing dropped lower than the other, the chances were likely that the fixed landing gear on the low-wing side would touch the water first, causing the aircraft to cartwheel and flip sideways. There was a gas tank to my immediate right, the top edge of the tank even with the side of my head. With the intense G-forces of a sudden deceleration, I would probably hit the side of my head against the edge of the tank and quite possibly be knocked out, or fracture my skull. Game over.

To compound the situation, I had decided that I would position my life raft, which was a bundle measuring 15 inches long, by 13 inches wide, by 10 inches high, in my lap, to use as a cushion, of sorts, to prevent me from hitting my head on the forward instrument panel. It had a lanyard mounted under a flap on the outside of the packet which could be extended prior to inflation. I would extend the lanyard far enough for me to tie the lanyard around my waist, thereby always staying 'attached' to the raft, should we become separated.

In order to have enough space in my lap to accommodate the size of the raft bundle, I would need to slide my seat all the way back. Unfortunately, this would make it impossible for my feet to operate the rudder pedals, which controlled the yaw, the left and right axis of the airplane. But more importantly, I would no longer be able to see over the aircraft's nose. With the gas tank to my right, and all of its radios mounted on top of the tank, I would be completely 'blind' to my right and straight ahead. I would only be able to see out the left window and the lower left corner of the windshield; not enough to tell when I would hit the surface of the water.

I needed to keep control of the remaining two control surfaces, the ailerons, which would help me keep the wings level, and the elevators, which allowed me to control the 'pitch' of the airplane for airspeed. If I could keep the wings level at touchdown, the plane should continue forward in a straight line, preventing me from hitting the side of my head against the fuel tank. I also needed to keep airspeed control to prevent a stall where I would then have no control. No. I decided against intentionally stalling the airplane. Instead, I would attempt a full flap landing just a few knots above the stall speed. This would give me the slowest possible speed while still keeping limited control.

I had access to the Cessna operating manual and reviewed the ditching procedure. I decided to modify some of the steps to fit my circumstances, and received approval from Earl and the Navy pilots. I read off each step to Earl, and added a few items of my own, and asked that he read aloud to me each step at the appropriate time. I did not want to perform the procedure from memory. We decided that once the engine quit, and my descent was initiated, Earl would fly in my five o'clock position and follow me down to the surface.

"Earl, if I get into the raft, I'll wave both arms to you. That means that I'm not hurt, the raft is in good shape, and you should continue on to Hawaii. If I get into the raft, and I only wave one arm, it means that I am banged up a little. Maybe a broken bone, or two, but basically, everything is okay. Keep going. If I get into the raft, and I do not wave to you, it means that I'm hurt pretty badly, I don't know how long I will last out there, and someone will probably have to get into the water with me if I am to survive."

I paused before continuing.

"And Earl, if I don't get into the raft, well... please tell my family that I love them, and I don't regret doing these flights. It is what I loved to do. And by the way, I want a raise."

It was around this time that we were contacted by the C-130 aircraft that had been on another mission near Oahu. Much of the conversation was between the P-3 and C-130, regarding their present locations, how long it would take the C-130 to get to my location, and what kind of equipment they had. Captain Piersig was trying to calculate if he should stay until the C-130 arrived, or if they should leave and continue on to San Francisco. They had just enough fuel to be able to make the California coast. But, if they stayed, they would have to return to Hawaii to refuel before going home. It also meant that they would have to shut down one of their four engines to conserve fuel. This crew had been away in the Sea of Japan for nearly five weeks. They were tired and they missed their loved ones.

By this time, I was getting to know the P-3 crew and was feeling fairly comfortable with the situation, in an odd sort of way. Some people, when faced with a tense situation can become terse, or abrupt. Some people become despondent. I discovered that when faced with an emergency, my way of coping is that I have a strange sense of humor. This back and forth between the C-130 crew and the crew of the P-3 went on for about 20 minutes. I broke into their conversation and said, "Finally, what I have always dreamed of, to have men fighting over me!"

Earl was of the opinion that the P-3 should probably go on to California, the C-130 would join up shortly.

Finally, Bill said, "Heidi... what would YOU like us to do?"

Normally, I would have deferred to Earl, but this was my life we were talking about.

"Well, I know you guys want to get home. But I would feel a whole lot better if you would stay until the C-130 has me in sight."

A voice came over the radio that none of us had heard before, saying, "ALRIGHT, HEIDI!"

'Who the hell was that?' I thought.

I didn't know it at the time, but the voice belonged to Captain Bob Stevenson. He and his crew, piloting a 747 for American Airlines, were flying overhead at 35,000 feet on their way from California to Hawaii. As was the standard operating procedure, they were monitoring 121.5, and heard all of the transmissions regarding my little 'problem.' His entire crew were crammed in the cockpit; the First Officer, Flight Engineer, Purser, and Flight Attendants. When an emergency is underway, it is prohibited for aircraft not involved in the emergency to break into transmissions. The channel must be kept open for essential aircraft only. But Captain Stevenson could not help himself. He and his crew were listening to the P-3 and C-130 crews debating whether the P-3 should stay, or go, and they were all yelling, "Make them stay, Heidi! Don't let them leave!"

"No problem, Heidi. We'll stay until the C-130 gets here. But Heidi?"

"Yes, Captain Piersig?"

"You owe me a beer."

Thirteen

Silence

"Earl, I've never had an engine fail before. What can I expect?"

"Oh, you'll know! There will be a lot of noise coming from the engine, some surging, the oil temp will probably be at red line. You'll know."

I took a glance at my oil gauges. The pressure was touching the zero line, but the oil temperature was still in the green, 'normal' range. Maybe it was just a bad sensor. I hoped that was the case. It had been over two hours since I made that initial Mayday call. It felt like it had been days. It felt like it had been minutes.

What was that? I felt an almost imperceptible deceleration, just for a second. Was it turbulence? There it is again! Maybe I'm imagining it.

A metallic 'tap-tap-tap,' a slight little shudder, and then...
Silence.

Fourteen

Beauty and the Beast

I know I should have been alarmed at the failure of the engine, maybe even panicked, but in those first few seconds, I was immediately struck at how incredibly beautiful the scenery was. The constant droning of an aircraft's engine detracts from appreciating your surroundings. The early afternoon sun sparkled golden on the water, almost painful to look at. The sky, a brilliant, crystal blue. The loudness of the engine was replaced by the soft purr of the windmilling propellor.

I was back in my days of glider flying. It was just a bit heavier, that was all. I set the Flaps to ten degrees for a better descent angle.

Airspeed–70 knots.

My descent had begun. Earl moved into my four o'clock position and let the P-3 crew know that I was starting down. They announced that they would be descending, as well.

It was time to get to work. I located everything loose I could find in the cockpit, and threw the items on the far side of the forward ferry tank, closest to the right door. When it came time to remove the kneeboard that was strapped around my thigh, I hesitated. It made me think of the first time I had used this device during my early days of flight training. More than likely, I would never see these items again. I thought about all of the other personal effects that would be lost; my wallet that contained pictures of family and friends, the first Temporary

Airman Certificate I earned for glider flying. I'd lose the diamond and sapphire ring Bob had given me, and a beautiful pink angora sweater I had just purchased on my last trip to New Zealand. But these items were stashed inside of my suitcase, and that was stowed in the tail of the airplane. I couldn't get to them if I wanted to. And, at the time, these things were low on the list of priorities that demanded my attention.

I slid my seat back, grabbed the handle on my life raft and it toppled into my lap. I was right. I couldn't reach the rudder pedals any longer, and could barely see the surface of the ocean out the front windshield. *Damn. Couldn't I have been wrong about this?*

I partially extended the lanyard from the side of the raft, and looped it around my waist, praying that it would be sturdy enough to withstand what was about to happen.

"Hey, Heidi," Bill Piersig said.

"Yes, Bill?"

"I have nine volunteers here that will be glad to get into the raft with you."

"GREAT! It might be a bit crowded, but tell them to come on down, and don't forget the six-pack!"

My sense of humor was still intact, but as the surface of the ocean got closer, it quickly evaporated. This was really happening now. I was wondering what was going to happen. The ocean, which had appeared so magnificent just a few minutes before, now resembled something menacing. And it was waiting for me.

Fifteen

Bob

Altitude – 4000 feet.

Airspeed – 70 knots.

The prop froze at a drunken angle. The windmilling had stopped. Now it really was quiet, only the sound of the wind for company.

Suddenly, I sensed a strange heat and pressure on both of my shoulders. It wasn't because of my shoulder harnesses, which had been tightened so much I would have had trouble sliding a pencil beneath them. And the sunlight streaming into the cockpit wasn't touching me.

The pressure and heat got more intense. It was as if someone was right behind me placing their hands on my shoulders.

I heard his voice, clearly and distinctly. But it wasn't coming from the 'outside.' And it wasn't as though I was imagining it. It was real.

Bob's laugh.

'Heidi, I'm right here with you. You are not alone. This is going to be a good experience and you'll be alright.'

I turned and looked at the picture of Bob, mounted on the side of the gas tank. I could imagine the way he would wink at me. Somehow, I knew that what he said was true. No matter what, I would be alright.

Yes. He was with me.

Sixteen

Fly The Airplane

As pilots, it is drummed into us from the beginning of our training, that whenever something goes wrong, be it insignificant, or serious, the first thing you do is:

FLY – THE – AIRPLANE.

Altitude 2,500 feet.

I had Earl start reading out loud the procedure we had worked up.

Fuel – Off. (I had no further need for it now, anyway.)

Electrical switches – Off. (I would now be on battery power, so I would still have the radios, at least for a while.)

Flaps – Full down.

Airspeed – 65 knots.

Heading – 260 degrees.

Altitude – 1,000 feet.

Window – Open. (Less resistance when moving the door through the water.)

Door – Crack open. (If the plane did cartwheel upon impact, the fuselage might twist and jam the door closed.)

"Earl, I'm still getting paid for this, aren't I?"

500 feet.

The ocean was right there!

"Earl, remember what to tell my family."

"Ah, hell, Heidi. You can tell them yourself when you and I are sipping beers in Hawaii tomorrow night!"

100 feet.

"Okay, Heidi. Master Switch off. Good luck."

Through the gap between the door and the forward wind-shield I could see the glassy surface of the water. It was so blue. It was SO close!

I don't want to do this. I DON'T WANT TO DO THIS!

I couldn't help but wonder what it was going to feel like. Surprisingly, I wasn't scared. But I think that all pilots, at one time or another, wonder how they will react if they ever have to experience a forced landing. At the last second, will they give up and brace themselves, or hold their arms up in front of their faces? Will they give in to their natural reflexes, or continue to FLY-THE-AIRPLANE?

I was looking out the left window, trying to judge my height above the water, when BAM! The main wheels touched the surface of the water. The plane skipped back up into the air, but immediately nosed over as I could feel the intense pressure of the shoulder harnesses pressing into my flesh. The nose wheel hit. As the plane pitched forward onto it's back, I remember hearing myself make an audible gasp, if not from the force of the deceleration, then from shock. In that inhalation, I had saltwater. It was an explosion of water in the cockpit. Within seconds I was on my back in an inverted 45-degree angle.

Both of my hands were still clutching the handles of the control yoke. I had not given up at the last second. I FLEW the airplane.

I could tell through my closed eyelids a sickly green-ish-brown-yellowish shroud. Is this what death looks like?

My first thought was, 'My God, I'm going to drown.'

Seventeen

Summer 1960

I was four years old. My family had been invited to a pool party at a friend's house a couple of hours away. They were good friends of my parents; so good, in fact, that their two teenage children, Sandy and Richard, ages 16 and 17, were named as our godparents.

The party was outdoors in their backyard, which was L-shaped. The pool was around back, secluded from where all of the tables were set up for eating. It was a fun group of around 20 guests in all. But Sandy was the person I was most looking forward to seeing. I adored her. She had two horses, and would take me riding occasionally. She, and her boyfriend Adam, had been working during the summer for the Red Cross.

My two sisters, Allison and Lisa, ages six and seven were enjoying the pool activities. Being shy, as I was, I spent most of the time with my mother. But the sounds of laughter coming from the pool area finally enticed me to investigate what all the merriment was about.

There was Adam, tossing a beachball to my sisters who were in the shallow end of the pool. What fun! I did not know how to swim, but sat on the edge of the pool and Adam would toss the beachball to me occasionally until it was time to eat.

We enjoyed the typical fare, burgers, hot dogs, potato salad and watermelon. There were several large picnic tables set up to accommodate everyone. I sat next to my sisters and some of the other children that were there. As everyone lingered over the food, I just couldn't let go of how much fun I had with that beachball. I quietly slipped away from the table and made my way back to the pool area.

There it was, just floating there, the plastic orb of white, red, and yellow, shiny from the water. It was near the corner of the deep end of the pool. Could I reach it? I bet I could if I stretched my arm out just…a…little…further.

I was in the water. I struggled to get to the surface for air, but my flailing just made matters worse. I was holding my breath, but I must have swallowed some water when I fell in. The taste of the chlorine burned my throat. Finally, I just couldn't hold my breath any longer. I desperately needed air! I was panicked! I took a breath. Water went up my nose and down my throat. It stung. It made me cough, which forced me to take another breath. This time it wasn't so bad. My lungs responded as though they were getting the oxygen they needed, but instead of breathing oxygen, I was breathing water. My third breath, and it felt pretty natural, but I was getting sleepy.

My eyes remained closed, but I could sense the pale blue color of the pool water through my closed eyelids. Beautiful. I was suspended, in a sort of limbo, the blue all around me. My surroundings started getting brighter; now a brilliant white, with just a tinge of blue. So calm. So peaceful. I could stay like that forever.

It seemed as though I had been suspended there for a long time. Off in the distance, I could barely make out a muffled noise of some kind. Was that yelling? Talking? Why don't they shut up?! Why don't they go away? I'm fine.

My mother was still enjoying her lunch, and the conversation with friends. She glanced at the table where I had been sitting with my sisters, but my place was empty. My half-eaten food still on the plate.

"Where's Heidi?"

My mother got up from the table and started searching. It didn't take long for someone to discover my body, face down on the surface of the pool. An air bubble was trapped in my bathing suit top. It was the only thing visible above the surface of the water. Within seconds, nearly all of the men had jumped into the water and pulled my body from the pool.

There was no pulse. No heartbeat. I was clinically dead.

In the late 1950's, it was still common practice for drowning victims to be placed on their sides, or stomachs, in an attempt to push the water out of their lungs by pressing down on their backs, although mouth-to-mouth resuscitation was the most commonly used procedure, and CPR had just been invented that year, but very few people were trained in its use.

A crowd of people hovered around me, frantic to help. Sandy and Adam appeared, and pushing everyone away from my lifeless body, started doing CPR, which they had just been trained to do at work. Just as the second fire truck arrived, I took my first breath. A small piece of watermelon was expelled that had been lodged in my throat which prevented excessive water from going into my lungs.

The faraway muffled sounds I was trying to ignore were getting louder. I was angry. Why wouldn't everyone just leave me alone? I finally opened my eyes to the blurry sights of people. What was a trampoline doing there? I don't remember it being there before. It was actually a gurney from the ambulance that had arrived a few minutes before, but everything appeared distorted to me. It was hard to focus. There was so much noise and confusion.

I don't remember much about the ride to the hospital, or the immediate aftermath. All I do know is that it took me years to get into a swimming pool after that. Of course, my parents tried to 'waterproof' me after my accident. But every time we visited the pool at our grandparents' community center, I would hang onto my father for dear life. I wouldn't let him let go of me. The best I could do was to sit in water that was only a foot deep. The sound of water going into my ears made my entire body stiffen and it would be difficult for me to breathe. For years, in order to wash my hair, my mother would have to fill the bathtub with only a few inches of water. She would climb in, cradle me in her arms, and I would dig my nails into her arm to make sure my head would remain above the water line, as she would gently and slowly pour water from a cup over my backward tilted head.

Each year, my parents would ship my sisters and me off to our grandparents' house for two weeks. Every morning while we were there we would go to the pool where my sisters would enjoy splashing around. I would immediately find a flotation ring, and spin around in the shallow end until it was time to leave.

One year, my grandparent's next-door neighbor, Mr. Hindman had offered to give swimming lessons to my two older sisters. He was retired from the Navy. It had been his job to teach swimming during basic training. He was aware of my history, and had a plan.

Each day, he would give swimming exercises to my sisters, and gushed praise for their attempts, and the progress they made. Not wanting to be ignored, I would say, "Look at me, Mr. Hindman! Look at what I can do!" as I would spin in circles with the inflatable doughnut around my waist.

Mr. Hindman stared at me, a blank look on his face.

"Heidi, until you can put your head under water for three seconds, I have nothing to say to you." And he ignored me for the rest of the morning.

I was crushed. I loved Mr. Hindman. We would play croquet in the backyard with him. He was normally so nice. I wanted to cry. Why was he being so mean to me?

The next morning at the pool, I was determined that I would win him back. Before Mr. Hindman arrived, I sat on the second step of the pool, held onto the edge of the rough tiles that surrounded the pool, and put my face in the water. It felt awful. I hated the smell. And when I sat up and opened my eyelids, the chlorinated water stung my eyes. But I just couldn't have Mr. Hindman ignore me again!

He arrived. He got busy instructing my sisters in various tasks. I got up my nerve and said, "Mr. Hindman." He ignored me. A little louder, "Mr. HINDMAN!" He glanced over to me, and with an exasperated look said, "Yes?"

This was the moment. I stood in the water, next to the side of the pool, my head just above the surface, placed both hands on the edge of the pool, and submerged my head. One – two – three seconds. I could hear Mr. Hindman yell, "That's GREAT, Heidi!"

Four – Five – Six – Seven – Eight – Nine – TEN!

I lurched upwards, wiped the water from my eyes, and saw the joy on Mr. Hindman's face.

Over the remainder of our stay, Mr. Hindman managed to teach me the dogpaddle, the sidestroke, and how to float on my stomach. There was no use in trying to teach me the conventional swimming technique, or how to float on my back. As soon as that water flowed into my ears, instinctively, I would sit upright. If there happened to be a lot of splashing near me in the water, I would tense up, and it would be hard for me to breathe.

The trauma of my pool accident stayed with me my entire life. But then, maybe things happen for a reason.

Eighteen

Farewells

It felt to me as though the plane was rapidly sinking. I was hanging upside down, underwater. *'GET OUT!'* I screamed inside my head. I tried moving but my seat belt and shoulder harnesses were holding me in place. I immediately flashbacked to my time in the swimming pool when I was four years old. Would I succumb to the peaceful bliss of allowing the water to take over?

I started yelling at myself in my thoughts. *GOD DAMMIT, HEIDI! NO ONE IS GOING TO JUMP IN AND SAVE YOU THIS TIME! MOVE!!*

My hands went down to unbuckle my seat belt, which would also release the shoulder harnesses. *Where is my raft? It was in my lap just a moment ago! Don't worry about that right now, just GET OUT!*

I was disoriented. I couldn't tell which way was up, right, or left. My eyelids were still clenched shut. I had never been able to open my eyes underwater. But I knew that there was a door on one side of me, and a gas tank on the other. I took my arms, held them against my sides, and pushed outward. Sure enough, my right hand connected with the side of the gas tank, and my left hand touched the door. I gave it a push, and could feel the slight resistance from the water, but the door swung open. I started to move in that direction. Even though my eyelids were shut, I could sense colors and light. Slowly, the putrid looking water evolved into a regular shade of dark blue, then fading to crystalline turquoise. I could tell that I was moving in the right direction! Suddenly a white flash, and the sunlight was bathing my face.

The P-3 had followed me down to about 200 feet above the surface. The crew watched tensely as my plane hit the water. They waited, some holding their breath.

"Get out, Heidi! Get out!" many of them yelled. Had I survived the impact? Their question was answered about 30 seconds later when they saw my head pop up.

With my plane resting upside down, what would normally be considered a 'high-wing' airplane, was now a 'low-wing' airplane. It provided me with the perfect platform to stand upon so I could retrieve my gear and maybe, the rest of my belongings. I noticed that the lanyard was still in place around my middle. I followed the length of the cord, and there it was . . . my beautiful little raft. It was floating inside of the cockpit. Of course, when the plane flipped over, the raft floated up to the surface and away from my lap. I managed to get up onto the underside of the wing, pull the raft towards me and found the inflation handle.

Two months earlier, I had taken my raft and supplies into a company in San Francisco that serviced and inspected survival equipment. This was standard operating procedure every year. The raft would be opened, inspected for leaks and tears, and the equipment gone over to make sure it was in good condition. What they found was that the CO_2 cartridge used to inflate the raft still had a charge, but not enough to fully inflate the raft. Fortunately, this was caught, and they replaced it with a new, fully pressurized cartridge. My particular raft had a floor, and one continuous 'ring' surrounding it. There was a definite top and bottom. If you have seen the movie, Castaway, with Tom Hanks, while my raft was packaged differently, once inflated, it was the same size and configuration as the one in the movie.

As I gripped the inflation handle, I said a silent prayer that the raft would come to life. I pulled and was greeted by a loud bang, and the whoosh of the raft filling with air. As happy as I was, I soon noticed that there was a problem. I realized that the raft was opening upside down. This was not good. If the raft fully inflated in the wrong position, I would have to 'right' it. In order to do that, I would have to lay face-down, spread-eagled, grip two fabric handles mounted on the underside of the raft floor, slip my feet into another two fabric handles, and then throw myself up and backwards, ending up underneath the raft in the water. No way did I want to attempt that!

I was still standing on the wing and was able to clumsily flip the raft into the correct position while it was still half limp. It worked. Within 15 seconds the raft was fully inflated and right-side up.

Just then I heard and saw Earl fly over. This had been his second pass since following me down to the surface. I could see his face, and he waved to me, but I was concentrating on getting myself into the raft first before initiating my 'signal' to him. And the adrenaline coursing through my system might be masking any injuries I might have sustained. I would wait to signal him back. I needed to get busy.

I pulled on the orange tabs of my military-issued life vest, but all that happened was that it opened and unfolded. No welcome hiss of air filling the vest bladder. 'Don't worry about that now! Get into the raft!'

A wave hit me, and I was knocked off the wing. Using my exceptional skill of the dogpaddle (Thank you, Mr. Hindman!), I splashed my way over to the welcoming raft and tried to get in. My shoulders and chest got as far as the top of the tube, but suddenly, I got pulled back into the water. I tried again. I positioned my chest as close to the raft as possible, placed both of my hands on the top of the tube, and pushed down, hoping to catapult me into the raft. Again, I got pulled back into the water. I looked down through the clear water and discovered that the lanyard was wrapped around one of my ankles. The cord must be caught somewhere to the airplane and every time I tried to get into the raft, the slack would be taken up and prevent me from securing my safety. It seemed that nothing was going according to plan.

I paddled back to the wing, as the raft was slowly drifting towards the tail of the airplane and away from the cockpit. I managed to get back up on the wing, but would fall over from the swells undulating beneath me. Mr. Hindman should have given me surfing lessons too.

Finally, I was able to disentangle myself from the web of the lanyard. By this time, the raft was at the rear of the airplane, close to the tail. It meant that I would have to jump back into the water and cover the distance of what seemed like a mile, back to the raft. I felt shaky and tired.

One more time. With every ounce of energy I had left, I pulled myself up and fell into the raft. I could have cried with the relief I felt at that moment. A loud roar came from the sky. I looked up and for the first time, saw the sleek, gray, white, and black P-3, the five-pointed Navy Star presented proudly on the side of the fuselage. They had always flown far above me before the engine quit. Seeing them fly over, knowing all that they had done for me, well... they were 'family' now. I knew that they must be happy seeing me safely in the raft.

I still needed to maneuver my raft back to the cockpit to see if I could retrieve the bag of extra survival equipment I carried. And if possible, maybe I could get my suitcase too. I did not have any oars packaged inside of the raft, so I leaned over the side and tried paddling to inch the raft closer to the cockpit, but I didn't seem to be moving very far. Then, I heard a faint scraping noise. Up until then, the only sounds I heard were the gentle slaps of water brushing up against the airplane, and the far-off hum of Earl's 172 and the P-3 crew flying nearby. What could be making that noise?

I turned my head to see that the raft was pinned against the rudder mounted on the aft side of the airplane's tail. The rudder was made of corrugated aluminum. The back edge of the rudder had rough edges that were extremely sharp. The image of a leaky balloon appeared in my head, flitting into the sky from the release of helium. Evidently, the lanyard, which had trapped me earlier, was now doing the same to my raft. The cord was so long, about 25 feet, that I could not see its entire length, and discover where it was hung up. I had no choice but to cut myself free. I had no idea of how long the plane would stay afloat. If it suddenly sank into the depths of the sea, it might pull the raft, and me, down with it.

Packaged inside of the raft, along with a couple of plastic bags containing varied supplies, were items mounted along the inside surface of the raft. Amongst these items was a knife. It was contained inside of a metal sheath, or container, that was taped to keep it closed. My hands were wet, and probably a bit shaky, as I struggled to free the knife from its container. It seemed to take forever before I had the knife ready to use. I noticed that the blade was as sharp as a flatware knife you would have at your dinner table. It was probably a wise idea not to have many sharp items when cruising around in a life raft, but really? I sawed away at the lanyard for at least a minute before it finally surrendered to my assault. The raft was free and fortunately, no damage had been done to the fabric of the raft.

Approaching ditching site, the dot at the center of the circle is my airplane

95

Earl made another pass, and I felt that I could finally signal to him that I was okay. I hadn't noticed any stabs of pain from broken bones. I didn't see any blood on my clothes, although I did feel as though I had gone a couple of rounds with Muhammad Ali. I was pretty sore.

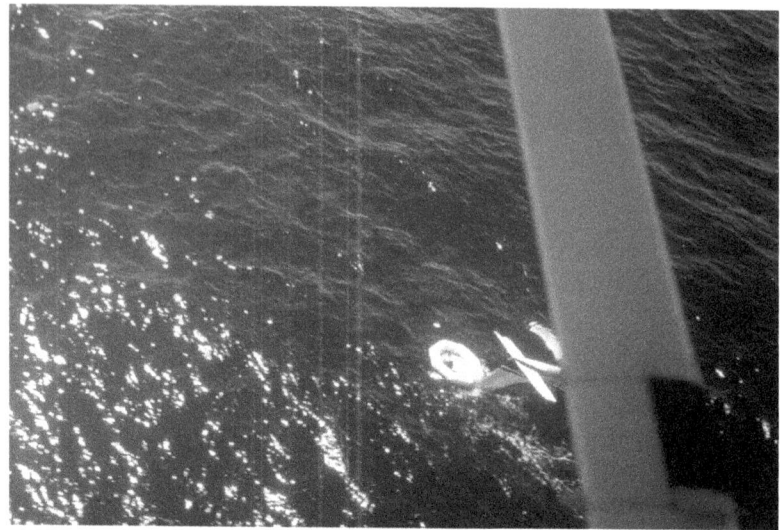

Raft pinned against rudder

As he came over, I raised both arms and waved them in as big of an arc as I could manage. He confirmed that he had understood my signal by rocking his wings. I watched him come around for one final pass before he took up a heading for Hawaii, and probably a cold beer.

Once I severed the lanyard, I could tell that I was immediately going to be drifting away from my airplane. I was no longer tethered to the raft. I had a choice to make. Stay put and be satisfied with the minimum amount of supplies packaged in the raft, or leave the raft, swim over to the plane, retrieve the bag of extra survival equipment, and hopefully, make it back to the safety of the raft.

At the time, it seemed like an easy decision to make. I had expended most of the energy I had in dealing with the problems up until that point. Did I really think I could make it to the cockpit and back, loaded down with supplies and be able to get myself back into the raft again? What if it drifted away faster than I was able to swim? Nope. I was going to stay put.

Lanyard has been cut, drifting away

I decided to take one more attempt at inflating my life vest. My first try was unsuccessful. Maybe the CO2 cartridge had gone bad. I took both of the inflation tabs in my hands and gave a yank. WHOOSH! I was startled as the vest burst into a cushion of air, hugging my neck and chest. It didn't take long for me to realize that had the vest inflated on the first attempt, it would have prevented me from the leverage I needed to get into the raft. Was that you, Bob?

I could see that the P-3 had climbed back up to around 1,000 feet. It flew in a wide circle while it waited for the Coast Guard C-130 to join up and take over. It shouldn't be too long now. But I was happy to have them nearby, just the same.

I glanced at my airplane. The weight of the engine was pulling the nose of the plane down farther into the water. It was no longer at a 45-degree inverted angle. It was more vertical. I was spellbound by the sight. It wasn't often that you saw an airplane in this position.

I was suddenly overtaken by an immense feeling of sadness. It may sound ridiculous, but I had always felt that airplanes have 'souls.' Some airplanes you like better than others. Yet, they each had their own personalities. And the type of flying we did over the ocean, bonding with a piece of machinery over the many, many hours of flight, well… your airplane was another crew-member. You took care of it, and it took care of you.

N8032M had seen me through this ordeal. It ran as long as it could. It didn't break up on impact. And now it was 'dying,' and there was nothing I could do about it. I had to look away. A few minutes later, I took one more look.

The entire front half of the plane was now underwater. I could see the underside of the aft half of the fuselage and tail.

It looked like a cross.

Nineteen

A Blessing in Disguise

Now, it was a waiting game for the C-130 to arrive and relieve the P-3. Captain Piersig made another call to the Coast Guard SAR center. Had the 'Alert' plane been dispatched yet? The answer was 'No.' They were probably waiting to hear if I had survived the ditching. No use in them wasting their resources if there was no one to rescue.

The P-3 continued its wide circling pattern for about 20 minutes before the Coast Guard C-130 appeared. A conversation ensued between the two crews as to fuel status. The C-130 had approximately two hours of fuel that could be used to stay 'on station' before having to head back to Hawaii to refuel. The P-3 had about the same, but they were a faster airplane than the C-130. They could conceivably boogie back to Hawaii, refuel, and make it back to my location before the C-130 would have to leave. It was settled. That's what they would do. But before the P-3 left, they decided to drop a sonobuoy in the water which would assist other aircraft and vessels keep track of my location by emitting a radio signal from the surface, and a hydrophone sensor below the surface.

A sonobuoy is five inches in diameter and three feet long. They are ejected from the aircraft in canisters along a chute. Normally, this isn't a problem. However, on this flight, there were three extra crew members, making a total of 13 souls on board with over a month's worth of luggage and cargo, making the confines of the aircraft extremely crowded. They had a difficult time maneuvering their way to the ejection chute. Three attempts were made to launch the sonobuoy. All failed. Capt. Piersig was getting frustrated and anxious. If a sonobuoy could not be deployed, it would be nearly impossible to relocate my tiny speck of a raft all over again.

One of the crew volunteered to throw the sonobuoy out the door of the aircraft. This was a dangerous endeavor. He could easily be sucked out of the plane in the slipstream. But there was no other choice. A tether was attached to the crewman. The door was opened, and a blast of air and noise filled the confines of the aircraft. Capt. Piersig made another pass over my raft and yelled over the intercom, "Now, Now, NOW!"

The canister was thrown out the door and wobbled its way down to the surface of the water. Mission accomplished. They could head for Hawaii.

During this time, the C-130 had made a few passes overhead. I waved each time they flew over. They started dropping smoke flares from the aircraft. The smoke from the flares would give an indication of the direction of the wind on the surface. This was valuable information for determining the best location for dropping supplies. A few minutes earlier I had dropped a packet of sea dye marker into the water with the hopes that they could see in which direction I would be drifting.

Suddenly, I saw two large bundles drop from the tailgate of the C-130. They consisted of a 30-man life raft and a separate bag of supplies. What was invisible to me was that the two bundles were connected by a long rope. The plan was that the packets would be dropped upwind of the target; me. The wind would carry the items towards my raft where I could grab the rope connecting the two items, pull them towards me, and 'Voila!' A 'Hilton' at my disposal. The supply packet might even contain a jukebox and a disco ball. But realistically, it would be beyond wonderful to have a much larger raft with a cover to protect me from the elements, and a stash of better supplies; water, food, possibly a radio.

C-130 dropping smoke flare to check wind direction, life raft at bottom

Coast Guard C-130, N8032M in vertical position, sea dye marker off left wingtip of Coast Guard plane

I watched, fascinated, as the bundles hit the water. They landed approximately a quarter of a mile away from where I was floating. I continued to watch the bundles bob up and down along with the swells. They did not present much of a profile against the horizon, and it didn't seem like they were moving any closer to me. Now what?

I had cut the only 'lifeline' I had to the raft. Could I some-how attach myself back to the raft by using the cord of the sea anchor, or something in the fishing kit to pull the raft behind me as I swam over to the new raft? Nothing I could find seemed very useful.

Overhead, Capt. Piersig had watched as the raft and supplies had been dropped. Most of the crewmembers were staring out of the windows, as well. Within 30 seconds, they realized what had happened.

"She's dead," one of them said out loud.

What the smoke flares could not account for was the strength of the current, which was moving in the opposite direction of the surface winds. They knew almost immediately that if I tried to swim for the new supplies, I'd never make it. From past rescue missions they had witnessed survivors of capsized boats attempt to swim in open water for another form of flotation, and had underestimated the challenges of swimming in the open waters of the ocean. Most times, they could not keep sight of the target within the swells, and get disoriented. They assumed that I would do the same thing, and drown.

As the distance slowly increased between my raft and what had been dropped, a minute passed, then three, then five. I hadn't moved.

I said to myself, *You know, I think I'm okay where I am right now. I have some supplies, even if they are minimal. I think I'll just stay put.* I knew my limitations when it came to swimming.

The crews of both the P-3 and C-130 were baffled as to why I had not attempted to swim for the new rafts, but they were grateful that I did not. They knew that I would have died if I had tried.

It was the last time that I ever regretted having fallen into that swimming pool.

Twenty

Stages

Now I felt alone.

The P-3 had taken up a heading for Hilo, and eventually, the C-130 was relieved by a different P-3 that had been diverted from another mission. Because of the placement of the sonobuoy, the P-3 could stay at a higher altitude and fly in wider circles. So, while they were there at my location, most of the time I could not see or hear them.

I looked at my watch. The hands of my Timex had frozen at 2:14 pm. How much longer would it be before I was rescued? The last radio communication I had received before going into the water was that a Navy destroyer was going to be dispatched from Pearl Harbor. But I knew that I was at least 500 miles from Pearl. I guessed that the cruising speed of a destroyer was probably around 25 knots. It looked like I would be spending the night at sea.

The adrenaline rush was starting to wear off. My muscles were sore from the ditching and the difficult task of getting out of the airplane and into the raft. I could feel heat radiating off of a massive bruise that I had sustained on the bicep area of my right arm. It was already developing into a mottled deep purple-black mound. Fortunately, that was my only injury, besides a few scrapes.

I stretched my legs out in front of me. Even though my raft was certified to hold four 'men,' there was not enough room for me to lay down without curling up on my side. And unfortunately, any low spot on the floor of the raft collected water. I attempted to bail out the water, but I was never able to get the last few inches where I sat thrown overboard. I was also concerned that if I laid down, the rescue crews might think I was ill. As I sat upright, water would slosh up my back every few seconds. It was annoying, to say the least.

I closed my eyes. I was tired, physically, emotionally, and mentally. Within minutes a wave of nausea swept over me. I swung my head over the side of the raft just in time before vomiting. When the airplane pitched over, I had swallowed a large amount of sea water. I had the briny taste in my mouth ever since, but now it was replaced with the sour aftertaste of vomit. Fortunately, I hadn't eaten since the afternoon before. There was nothing to drink packaged inside of the raft, but I did have a solar still that could make water through condensation. That would be a long process.

After I splashed sea water on my mouth to wash away any remnants of... you know, I stared down into the water. It was blue with just a twinge of green, and so clear that it was hard to focus, knowing that the depth of water exceeded 20,000 feet. I was over the Hawaiian Trough Northeast Pacific Basin. I became hypnotized until after a minute I started to experience vertigo. After that, I could not look down into the water for more than a few moments.

I tried to remember what I had read in the Air Force Survival Manual regarding tips on how best to survive at sea. I remembered that it mentioned that after experiencing a traumatic event, you should refrain from eating or drinking for the first 24 hours. No problem. I found that I wasn't hungry or thirsty, other than trying to get rid of the bad taste in my mouth. I knew that I was in shock. Even though I was perfectly calm, I think that my mind and body were busy dealing with the trauma of the event. I was subconsciously 'load shedding' everything I could in order to deal with the situation. I was surprised at my detached comportment.

Heidi, you've just been through an ocean ditching. You're hundreds of miles from land, and you have no idea of when, or if, you will be rescued. You should be crying! is what I thought. I tried to work up some type of emotion, but I was numb.

I decided to get acquainted with the supplies that I had with me. I found two plastic bags full of odds and ends. One of the bags contained a towelette that I used to keep on top of my head to prevent sunburn. There was a small, cylindrical accordion-style pump that screwed into a port on the tube of the raft for adding air. I quickly did an inspection to make sure there were no active air leaks. All good. A fishing kit, signal mirror, the sea dye marker I had already used, water collection bag, first aid kit, wrist compass, and two space blankets rounded out the collection. In the other bag was the sea anchor, which could double as a bailing bucket, flashlight, one parachute flare, leak-stopper kit, and a whistle, which was on a thick fabric cord. I put the whistle around my neck, and deployed the sea anchor to minimize my drift.

I took in my surroundings. It was a beautiful day; sunny, blue skies with just a few 'cotton ball' clouds. The winds were light, and the temperature was in the low 80's, for which I was grateful. My clothes were wet, and I was hoping that my upper torso would dry out before the sun descended below the horizon. There was nothing I could do about getting my pants to dry out. I would be sitting in water for the duration.

It suddenly occurred to me that I had lost all of my belongings. What a hassle it was going to be to replace my licenses, credit cards and other documentation. The clothes didn't matter. Well, except for that luxurious angora sweater! I would miss my beautiful ring, the gift from Bob. I even thought about the Aviation Circular Computer I had used ever since I was a student pilot. It was a sort of slide rule that pilots used for flight planning. It was made of thick cardboard, but I refused to trade it in for one of the fancy metal jobs. But mostly, I was mad at myself for not removing the photo of Bob that I had taped to the forward ferry tank. Why hadn't I taken that with me?

Another spasm of nausea was about to hit. I could feel it building. And then, an odd thing happened. I suddenly remembered a documentary I had seen, perhaps in the late sixties. It was 'The Undersea World of Jacques Cousteau – Sharks.' In the documentary, they described how sharks could home in on just a few drops of blood from hundreds of meters away.

'Where did that come from? How in the hell did I remember THAT?'

Had I sustained any internal injuries in the ditching? I didn't know, but I worried about putting any bodily fluids into the water. Yes, I wanted company, but not the man-eating kind. I mean, I was probably safe anyway. I suspected there weren't any sharks in the area because I never heard that music (Dah – Dum). But just the same, I emptied one of the plastic bags, cramming the supplies into the second bag just in time to wretch into the now empty bag. I immediately felt better.

Time passed. Eventually, I saw another C-130 appear. They dropped another sonobuoy and some supplies that never reached me. I was frustrated that there were no oars in the raft. On one pass, at a fairly low altitude, I could see that the 'tailgate' was down on the back end of the plane. Two crew members sat on the ramp, their lower legs hanging over the side. I waved, and they waved back. So close and yet so far! After a few minutes, they disappeared. I guess having the sonobuoys allowed them to stay in the general area without having to keep me in sight all of the time. I secretly hoped that one of them would lose their balance, and fall into the water to be with me.

I still couldn't sleep. So, I just sat there trying to occupy my thoughts with trivial matters when all of a sudden something 'snapped' inside my gut. I didn't even feel it building. I realized how badly I wanted to be on dry land. I started screaming with everything I had.

"GET ME OUT OF HERE! I DON'T WANT TO BE HERE ANYMORE! PLEASE, SOMEBODY HELP ME! AHHHHHH!"

And I let out a long, 'no-holds-barred' wail of exasperation, worry, and yes, fear. It occurred to me that it was probably the first time I had screamed like that, with such intensity, since I had been a toddler. It lasted for several minutes. The release of all of that pent up emotion made me feel better.

I watched the ocean and could see how it was changing color with the sun sitting lower on the horizon. I worried about my family and what they must be going through. I was sure that they had gotten word by now that I had gone down, that my location was known, that I was physically okay, and that help was on the way. I was glad that our family friends were there to help distract them.

I dozed a little bit, but the nausea was still making occasional visits. The smell of the warm rubber raft didn't help matters.

With the rhythmic sounds of the water kissing at the side of my raft, I fell into a trance-like state. And then it hit me.

This is where Bob went down!

I turned my head, and 20 feet away from me, sitting in the water, was a brown seagull. I had not seen him flying nearby, and he didn't make any screeching seagull sounds. He was just sitting there, staring at me.

A warm wave of peacefulness washed over me, and it was then that I remembered what I heard while the plane was going down. I was not alone. Bob was watching over me, and I felt that I would be alright.

We continued to stare at one another for the next ten minutes, and then he flew off.

Twenty-One

Game Over

I watched as the sun began to sink towards the horizon. Hawaii was out there somewhere. Had Earl made it to Hilo yet? Was he helping to get me rescued? How long had I been out here? I couldn't tell.

The P-3 had overflown Earl going into Hilo. While they arranged to have their aircraft refueled, Captain Piersig got on the phone to the Coast Guard Search and Rescue Command Center at Barbers Point to see what was being done to pick me up. He wanted to know if it would be necessary for them to go back 'on station.' They were told that they would not be needed as an Alert plane had finally been dispatched. Bill and his crew would be happy to be finally going home, but there was a sense of disappointment as well. They had a vested interest in the outcome of my rescue attempt. It would be hard for them to 'hand it over' to others. Fortunately, their route of flight would be taking them directly over my location, so they would at least be able to listen in on the efforts to pick me up.

It was now sunset. There was a line of towering cumulonimbus clouds on the horizon, and to the south were some isolated rain squalls, but they remained several miles away from me. It was getting cold, and the wind was picking up. What had been two-foot swells that afternoon were now developing into six-to-eight-foot swells. I knew I was going to be spending the night out here. How much worse was it going to get? When I departed California, the weather forecast had been good, but that was assuming I would have arrived at my destination hours earlier. I did not know what to expect now. It was getting tiring to constantly be worrying about another adverse development.

Planes had come, off and on, during that time to drop more sonobuoys, and possibly more supplies, but as was the case, the supplies never reached me.

I watched as the moon started its ascent from behind the clouds. The full moon had been the night before, so it was nearly a perfect orb on this evening. I thought back to the first time I had witnessed the beauty of a moonrise over the ocean. This one was no different in its magnificence. At the precise moment that it peeked over the top of the clouds, I had to close my eyes momentarily at its brilliance. Again, I felt sorry for those that had never seen an ocean moonrise before.

I was resigned to the fact that I would be out here all night. I decided that I had better 'batten down the hatches,' so to speak. I didn't want anything to be tossed out of the raft in case the swells got worse, so I tied down everything I could, including myself, to whatever I could find to anchor myself. I removed the two space blankets. My clothes never did dry out, and I continued to sit in about five inches of sea water.

The space blankets were made of a mylar-type material, silver on one side and copper on the other. They were thinner than the thickness of stiff cellophane. I attempted to wrap one of them around my legs, and the other around my torso. I soon discovered that the slightest wisp of wind would find its way into the tiniest crevice and whip the blanket into the air. It was impossible to find any relief. I finally gave up trying. The water was cold, and I began shivering uncontrollably.

About an hour later I saw the strobes of a P-3 coming towards me. Then, another one soon followed. They started dropping flares that exploded into incredible brightness as they slowly floated down to the surface, taking at least several minutes for their descent. It was a fascinating sight. Interspersed with the parachute flares were smoke flares. The two planes continued to circle around me dropping new flares as the previous ones died out.

Did this mean that a ship was nearby?

By this time, two more C-130s had joined the effort. The planes would fly in wide circles, several miles in diameter, but frequently they would fly directly overhead at a low altitude. I would signal to them with my flashlight. What I did not know at the time was that they had infrared cameras onboard. They could see me clearly. Maybe they were checking to see if I was still alive.

This practice of dropping flares continued for another hour before I saw it; a bright pinpoint of light directly on the horizon. I could only see it briefly, every 20 seconds, or so, when I was on the crest of a swell. Could I be imagining it? After all, I hadn't slept in nearly two days.

It took another 45 minutes before it stopped its progression, about a mile from my raft, but was close enough for me to make out the outline of a ship. Having been a World War II buff, and having seen just about every war movie from the 50's, 60's and 70's, I could tell that it was not the destroyer that had been promised. It was a cargo ship of some kind. Who cared! It was a miracle. My miracle.

I could make out that there were two searchlights on the deck, one forward and one aft. But most of the time they were pointed in the wrong direction. I had the one parachute flare in my lap, but I did not want to fire it if the crew was looking away from me. I waited. Finally, both searchlights were aimed in my direction, even though I was beyond the scope of their illumination.

I fired.

The flare exploded up into the sky and lit up. Yippee! Now all I had to do was wait a few minutes for them to come alongside and pick me up! It's over!

Nothing happened.

Then, to my horror, I realized that the ship was moving AWAY from me! NO!

I started screaming through my tears, "I'M HERE! I'M HERE! DON'T LEAVE ME! PLEASE DON'T LEAVE ME!"

The swells were nearing ten feet by now, and waves would occasionally splash more water into the raft. I was wet, sitting in water, and my shivering was getting more intense. I feared that in another half hour I would capsize and drown.

I vomited.

Twenty-Two

Best Laid Plans

Bill Piersig, and the crew of P-3 PQ857, were just coming up on the outskirts of my location on their way home to California. They listened to the radio chatter between the search and rescue planes and a vessel, the USNS Meteor that was in the area looking for me, Captain Frank Ballard in command.

P-3: "Meteor, we've been dropping flares around her location. Do you see them?"

Meteor: "Uh, yeah. We see some out there."

The delay in receiving transmissions was a nuisance. The radio operator was several decks below the main deck. He would receive the transmission, and then radio up to the bridge where they would disburse the information to the men on board, which happened to be every single crewmember. They each had a pair of binoculars 'glued' to their eyes. It would then take a couple of minutes before the radio operator was assessed of the situation that he could radio back to the airplanes.

P-3: "Look, if you just turn to the right a little bit, she'll be right in front of you."

The Meteor made a slight turn to the right. After a couple of minutes, they reported that they still did not see me.

P-3: "She's right there! Turn to the right some more."

Nothing. One more request was made to the Meteor to turn to the right.

Meteor: "Hey, we've ended up doing a 360-degree right turn. We still don't see her."

Captain Piersig looked at his co-pilot. Something was wrong. This wasn't making sense. They were tempted to turn around to see if they could help. They had become 'attached' to me and did not want to hear later that I had died.

C-130: "Okay… We are going to drop a line of flares. She is going to be at the end of that line."

Twenty-Three

Where's a Diplomat When You Need One

The ship stopped. It appeared that it had moved only to look in another area. They were maybe two miles away now.

The circling stopped and a line of new flares were dropped, bringing one of them very close to my raft, closer than any of the others had been.

What was that? Some kind of thrumming noise. I couldn't tell where it was coming from. Within a few minutes I could surmise that it was the sound of a launch, or whaleboat, nearby, but I couldn't see it.

I had no more flares. I had a signal mirror, but that was meant to use during daylight hours. My flashlight lens was full of water. My whistle! Blow the damn whistle!

If you've ever seen the famous jazz trumpeter, Dizzie Gillespie, that is who came to mind. When he played, his cheeks would expand to the point where you thought he was storing two billiard balls in his mouth, one in each cheek.

I took a deep breath, as much as I could considering that my heart was pounding out of my chest. I blew so hard that I thought my cheeks would tear open. I listened. I blew again, and again.

The sound of the motor was getting louder. There! Just a few swells away I could see the boat! It was headed straight for me!

C-130: "Meteor, I see your whaleboat in the water. She's right off your port side."

Long pause.

Meteor: "We don't have a whaleboat in the water."

C-130: "Well, SOMEONE has a whaleboat in the water. We see Heidi. She's onboard."

Captain Piersig and his crew were speechless. What had happened? Who were these guys? It didn't matter. Heidi was safe and they could go home in good spirits.

The boat, about 25 feet in length, pulled up within a few feet of my tiny raft. Two men threw me a line. I missed it. On the third attempt, I was able to grab it and pull my raft to the side of their boat. They grabbed me under the arms and pulled me up. I attempted to give one of them a hug, but his manner was disciplined and distant. No matter. I was safe. As ecstatic as I should have been, I was emotionally drained. It didn't really register to me that my ordeal was over.

They escorted me down a couple of steps into the interior of the boat, which had a roof and two long benches, one on each side of the compartment that ran the length of the area. I sat down, trying to make heads or tails out of what language they were speaking. There was a lot of confusion. Portuguese? No. Polish? No. German? Definitely not. Finally, I gave up. I pointed the index fingers of both hands at my chest and said, "American." Then I turned towards my bench mate and pointed at his chest.

"Russki."

Oh shit.

Twenty-Four

The 'Not So Cold' War

It was 1984. The Cold War had started two years after the end of World War II, 1947, and lasted until 1991. I was being taken to a Soviet ship. My mind raced. Would I end up in a gulag in Siberia? Would I be sold on the black market and end up a sex slave in some God-forsaken country, never to be heard from again? Within seconds, my 'better angels' told me to calm down, that it was just my exhaustion getting the better of me, and to be grateful that I had been rescued.

One of the men, Jorge, who had pulled me out of the raft motioned for me to take off my life vest. He removed the shirt he was wearing and put it around me. Then he gave me one of their life vests to wear. He sat across from me and steadied my legs as the launch crashed against the waves towards the ship.

It took about ten minutes to reach their ship, the 'Ussuriiskaya Taiga.' Pulleys were used to raise the boat up to the main deck. Before my second foot could touch down upon the steel decking, a woman, and Andre, the second man that had helped me out of the raft, briskly and firmly escorted me down five flights of stairs and into a medical examination room. The room was quite spartan, a desk, chair, a small cot, and a glass medicine cabinet.

In short order, I understood that the woman was a doctor. She was in her 50's, light-colored hair pulled back into a bun, no make-up. She pointed to herself and said, "Natasha." What else, right? I told her my name and she motioned for me to sit in the chair.

She went to work. She felt my skull for bumps and cuts, looked into my eyes, felt my limbs, taking a few moments longer to examine the large bruise on my right arm, and looked for any indications from me that I was in pain. She listened to my heart, tapped on my back, and seemed satisfied that I appeared to be unharmed.

She went to the medicine cabinet and took out a small, brown-colored glass vial with a rubber dropper attached. She had a very small glass of water, almost like a shot glass and placed about ten drops of dark brown fluid from the dropper into the water, then thrust it towards my face.

Was I supposed to drink this stuff? What if it was a liquid version of sodium pentothal? Were they going to torture me and wriggle my military secrets out of me?! My 'better angels' reappeared. 'Heidi, you don't have any military secrets. Drink the stuff.'

I drank. It tasted awful, like iodine. I waited for the room to start spinning, for me to sink into a state of oblivion. Nothing.

A younger woman came into the room carrying the thickest, softest sweatsuit I had ever seen. It was powder blue. I had been suffering from wet clothes clinging to me for the past ten hours. My abdomen muscles were sore from the hours of shaking and shivering. What I wouldn't give to feel some comfort on my skin and any kind of warmth. I didn't have to wait long. Natasha motioned for me to get out of my wet things and to put on the sweatsuit. She didn't need to 'tell' me twice. As her back was turned, I quickly got out of my clothes and into the sweat suit. It felt like I was wrapped in a warm cloud. It was heaven.

The examination over, Natasha escorted me out of the room and down the hall into another room. It had a single bed, a desk and chair, a coat rack, and an adjoining bathroom. She led me into the bathroom, and there was the biggest porcelain clawfoot bathtub I had ever seen. Steam rose from the hot water that filled the tub. While the last thing I wanted to do was to get out of the warm clothes they had given me, the idea of slipping into that warm water won the day.

I was waiting for Natasha to leave and give me some privacy, but she insisted on holding my arm while I undressed. Maybe she was afraid that I might have a concussion, and be unsteady on my feet, or that I wasn't used to the rolling of the ship on the high seas. I wasn't going to argue with her.

She helped me into the tub, and I can't even describe how wonderful it felt. I could feel the soreness and tightness in my body begin to relax. It was then that I noticed just how banged up and bruised I was. I couldn't remember the impacts that had caused such ugly bruises. Natasha handed me a bar of soap, a washcloth, which was more like a thick piece of gauze, and left the room, closing the door behind her. At last. I was safe, I was warm. I was alive.

After a few minutes, I decided that I would make an attempt at washing my hair. It was matted with salt, and who knows what else. I'm sure that when I was underwater immediately after the ditching, oil and grease from the engine created a film on the top of the water. But, how to wash it? I was used to washing my hair by leaning over the kitchen sink and maneuvering my head underneath the faucet. This would be a bit more challenging.

I was leaning forward, cupping my hands to pour water over my head, being careful not to get any water in my ears when I heard the door open. I was startled. I was hoping it wouldn't be some stranger, meaning some 'man.' It was Natasha. She took one look at what I was doing and kneeled down next to the tub. She placed her hand on the back of my neck, took the bar of soap from me, and plunged my head under the water. I came up sputtering for air to feel her rubbing the bar of soap over the crown of my head.

My God, I thought. *I've survived nine and a half hours at sea in a fucking life raft, and now I am going to be drowned in a bathtub!*

The torture didn't last long, thankfully. She left again and I proceeded to get dressed back into the wonderful sweatsuit. It felt even more sublime because now I was clean. Just as I was about to exit the bathroom, I heard new voices. I entered the bedroom to find not only Natasha, but two men.

The younger of the two men spoke. "Hello," he said in a Russian accent so thick, I could barely understand him. "I am the radio operator of this vessel. This is the captain," as he pointed to the stern looking man standing near the door.

I turned to the captain and nodded. He made a curt nod back.

The younger man continued. "We were following flares when we found you. We are headed for the Far East. You will be going with us."

No! Now I knew I would end up in some opium den, never to see my family again!

"Can't you just drop me off in Hawaii?"

"Nyet."

They left the room. I tried to calm my anxiety. I knew that the crews of the American rescue planes saw me being picked up. Maybe they would be able to coordinate something. One thing at a time.

Someone appeared with a tray of food. I sat on the bed, and Natasha brought the tray to me. On it was a cup of hot tea, and a plate with toast, two slices of very thick, greasy bacon, and four eggs. I took one look at the eggs, which had probably been fried a total of 30 seconds, as the whites were mostly raw and translucent. The aroma made my stomach turn. I was still feeling the nausea from all of the sea water I had swallowed. I tried to motion to her that if I ate the food, it would come back up. She got a strange look on her face. Later, I found out that the Russians get only one egg a week. They were rolling out the red carpet for me, and I turned my nose, literally, at it. If I had known that at the time, I would have forced them down.

I tentatively took a piece of the toast, and the cup of tea. I bit off a tiny bit of the toast, and when tasting the tea found that it had been prepared with at least three heaping spoonfuls of sugar. But it tasted and felt amazing.

Natasha took the tray from me, and tucked me into bed. She turned off the overhead light, shut the door, and then I heard the click of the door being locked from the outside. This alarmed me at first. Was I going to be a prisoner? But then I thought that not only was it supposed to prevent me from wandering around the ship, but it would also keep others out.

I closed my eyes, but sleep would not come. Too much had happened in such a short amount of time. And yet, it also felt like the last few hours were, in fact, days.

About 45 minutes passed. I heard some footfalls coming down the hall. There was a soft knock on the door, and I said, "Come in."

It was the radio operator again, and Natasha.

"We are in contact with an American ship in the area. We are going to transfer you. They will be here in less than an hour."

He left before I could tell him how much I had appreciated all that the captain and crew had done for me. Perhaps I would get the chance to see the captain before I left.

Natasha approached me and in her outstretched hands were my clothes, which had been washed, but not dried. They were very damp. Damn. Does this mean I have to give the sweatsuit back? She motioned to me that after I got dressed, I should walk back to her office. I nodded my head that I understood.

My old clothes were hard to put on, as they stuck to my skin. They made me shiver. But I managed to get them on, and reluctantly, placed the sweatsuit on the bed.

I made my way down the hall to Natasha's office. I noticed that there were many posters on the corridor walls. They were cartoonish drawings of fruits and vegetables and the proper way to wash and store them. Apparently, this was a refrigeration vessel carrying produce. Maybe this wasn't a Soviet spy ship with ballistic missiles for cargo, like I had imagined.

Waiting for me in Natasha's office , along with Natasha were

Jorge and Andre. The mood was much changed. Before, there was a tenseness in the air. Who was I? What was I doing out there? Had I come from a boat, a cruise ship, an airplane? Where was I going? People seemed unsettled at not knowing the answers to these questions.

Now that they had been in touch with the American ship, it was a much more relaxed atmosphere. Even though no one in the room spoke English, we made the best of it and tried to communicate, as if we were playing a game of charades.

At one point, Andre turned to me and said, "Reagan?"

Not wanting to cause a political faux pas, I took my hand, placed it flat in the air, palm down, and waggled my hand back and forth, as if I was non-committal. I returned the question with one of my own. "Olympics?" I queried.

In 1980 President Carter had announced that the U.S. would boycott the Olympic Games scheduled to take place in Moscow later that summer. This came after the Soviet Union failed to comply with Carter's deadline to withdraw its troops from Afghanistan. Four years later, the Soviet Union announced that it would not compete in the 1984 Olympics in Los Angeles. I could sense from Andre's expression that he was sad about this.

They brought out a map of the world and pointed to where each of them lived; Vladivostok, St. Petersburg, and Moscow. They wanted me to show them where I lived. I went straight to the California coast, and expected to see a word that looked like 'San Francisco,' but it wasn't there. In its place was some strange word that I could not identify. But I knew it was one and the same, so that's what I pointed to. They seemed pleased.

There was a piece of paper and a pencil on the table. Natasha pointed to me and then wrote the number 18, indicating my age. I said, "Nyet," crossed out the '18' and replaced it with '28.'

"NYET!" they all responded as they shook their heads back and forth. I suppose I did look like a drowned rat.

This game continued. Pointing to my ring finger, and then to each of them, I surmised that only one of them was married.

I held my flat hand at different heights to indicate 'children?' Surprisingly, we were able to find out quite a bit about one another.

Natasha looked at me sideways, her eyebrows low over her eyes. And in a serious tone, she said, "Spirits?"

Not being a 'tea totaler' by any means, as I'm an airport bum and used to being around 'the guys,' I nodded my head up and down, chuckled, and replied, "Da."

She left the room and came back a few minutes later with a couple of small tins, the same size as pineapple cans and some drinking glasses. She also carried a very large mason jar. On the jar's label was a picture of pears.

The small tins contained vodka. I guess glass can break while at sea. Vodka was precious cargo and had to be protected. She opened one of the tins and poured some vodka into each of four glasses. Each of us took one. I watched as each person downed the fluid in one gulp. Not wanting to be outdone, and to prove that 'we Americans can hang with the best of 'um,' I followed suit.

My throat felt as though it had ignited. Had I just swallowed lighter fluid? I couldn't breathe. Everyone in the room howled with laughter. I would have laughed too if I could only catch my breath. Natasha poured another round, but this time, she gave me a small glass of the pear juice. I'd take a sip of the vodka, and then alternate it with some of the juice.

She reached towards me and cradled between her fingers a charm that I wore around my neck on a gold chain. It was a charm of a Norfolk Island pine tree from Norfolk Island. It was the first thing that Bob had ever given me, and I wore it always. I could tell that she thought it was nice. The proper thing to do would have been to give it to her as a token of my appreciation, but I just couldn't bear to part with it. Looking back, I am deeply regretting that I did not remove the charm from the necklace, and give her the chain. I'm sure she would have been overwhelmed and grateful.

Then, Natasha took a key from a chain worn around her neck. She opened her desk drawer and inside was a petty cash box. She placed it on the desk, used the key to turn the lock, and opened the box. Inside was a single chocolate bar. She unwrapped the foil, broke off four pieces and gave one to each of us. This was a treasured treat. This I did not turn down.

Jorge had left the room for a short while, and when he returned, he motioned for me to sit down. He stood in front of me, his hands hidden behind his back. When he brought his hands forward, he was holding some cards, similar to small postcards, and a small ceramic bowl.

Gift cards of pottery pieces

There was a separate greeting card with a typed message on the inside. It read,

> *Pacific Ocean*
> *12 August 1984*
> *Ussuriiskaya Taiga*
> *Vladivostok, USSR*
> *WE WISH YOU GOOD HEALTH*

And it was signed by Natasha, Jorge, and Andre.

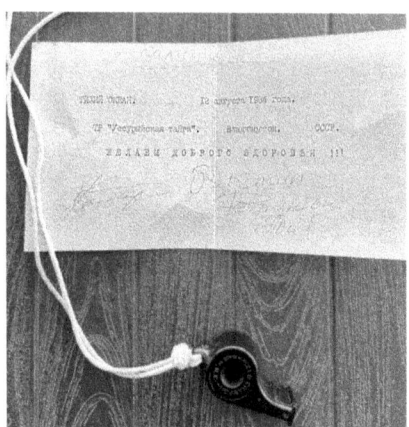

Inscription from Soviets, whistle

The other cards were a set of pictures of various pieces of ceramic artwork, bowls, plates, and vases. The small bowl was exquisite. In colors of brown, yellow, and black with a glossy glaze, it had a rustic pattern embossed into the ceramic. To this day, it is one of my most treasured possessions.

It was time to go. We all made our way up to the main deck. I could see my countrymen's ship in the distance. It was a cargo ship, and I was anxious to meet the crew.

There were approximately 20 crew surrounding me. I am sure they were curious as to who this stranger was that interrupted their normal routine. I was surprised to see that about a quarter of the crew were women. The deck had a party atmosphere. They were all smiling, and I waved to many of them. Natasha came over and gave me a huge bear hug. I had survived the ditching with no broken bones, but her hug came close. Then she kissed me on both cheeks. I could feel my throat constricting with emotion.

A crewman approached me and gave me some gloves to wear. They were made of a soft open-knit twine material. There were no embellishments, and I assumed they were used to work on the deck, possibly handling ropes.

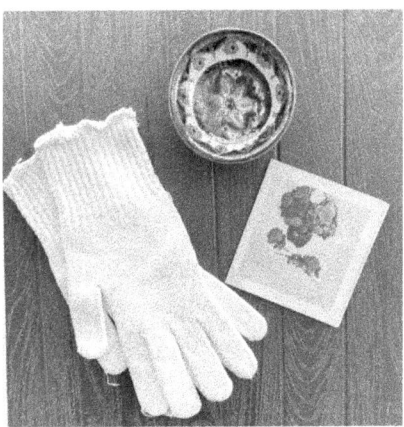

Gifts from Soviet crewmen

He then appeared with a wide fiberglass belt with padding on the inside. Around it, were metal loops. I was supposed to wear this around my middle, and they would hook a rope onto one of the loops. The problem was that when I stepped into the belt, raised it up to my waist and let go, it quickly fell to the floor. This caused a lot of laughter. I motioned to them that maybe I could hold it over my chest just underneath my armpits. But they waved their hands erratically in the negative. Eventually, they managed to secure it tightly around my waist. Then, I was supposed to lower myself down webbing that was placed along the side of the ship, much like what you would see in World War II movies when troops would lower themselves into the boats that would take them to the beach heads of battle. A launch would be waiting for me from the American ship at the water line.

I was disappointed. I had hoped that I would be able to go across in one of those chairs suspended on cables between two ships. It seemed like it might be fun. But the seas were still very rough. It must have been too dangerous.

Someone appeared with a camera and wanted to take my picture. He was just about to push the button, when I stopped him and motioned for Natasha, Jorge, and Andre to come over for a group photo. What I would have given to get a copy of that photo.

It was time. I climbed up onto a gap in the railing, turned around, found my footing in the webbing, and just before my head disappeared below the level of the deck, I took one final look at the smiling faces and the tears in Natasha's eyes, and said, "*Spasibo*," the one word I had asked to learn while on board.

Thank you.

Twenty-Five

Questions Answered

O nce I was about halfway down the webbing, I heard a booming voice coming from the launch below.

"My God! She's just a kid!"

I continued to make my way down, being careful with the placement of my feet and hands, as the boat would rise and fall with each swell. Suddenly, I felt two strong hands take hold of my waist, and I was pulled into the arms of two seaman. One slapped me on the back, while the other unhooked the belt from around my middle so it could be pulled back up to the deck of the ship. I was then given a life preserver to don, and someone wrapped a blanket around me.

They were all yelling greetings of some sort, and there were cheers coming from the Russians up on deck. I took a seat on one of the benches in the open 'whaleboat,' and as we slowly pulled away from the Soviet ship, I waved my arms in farewell. Natasha, Jorge, and Andre had their arms around each other.

"Boy, I bet you're glad to get off *that* ship!" one of the eight seamen said.

If they had asked me that question when I first got on board the Soviet ship, I might have agreed with them, but what could I say now that they would understand? It only took a short time for me to realize that once you remove all politics, people are generally good, and they will help a person in need with kindness and generosity. I'm sure it would have been quite the adventure to have spent more time with them. Just the same, I was happy to be getting back to the company of my countrymen.

This launch was about the same length as the boat that the Russians used, but it was open with several benches running the width of the boat. In the aft was a large, contained engine. I was told it would take about twenty minutes to make our way back to the U.S. ship. They told me how glad they were to see me and that I was okay. They seemed to be very interested in my story, and they were all asking questions at the same time. I did my best to address each question when I started to smell something. Then the conversation got quiet.

I could see that the men were all looking towards the back of the boat. I turned to see hazy, gray-purplish smoke wafting up from the engine compartment. Oh… my… God. 'What next?' I thought. The seaman at the stern was busy investigating the cause of the smoke, but in short order it was decided to shut it down and break out the oars. Suddenly, the jovial nature of the men mutated into silence. From the looks on their faces, I could read their minds. 'Do we really want to bring *her* on board *our* ship? Is she bad luck?' Fortunately, they did not take a vote to see if I should be thrown overboard.

We finally reached the side of the USNS Meteor, and was pulled up to the main deck on a set of pulleys. A male steward met me as I stepped out of the launch. We made our introductions, and then he told me that the captain would like to see me. On the way up to the bridge, the steward explained to me that I was on, what was known as, a 'gray ship,' Navy owned, civilian crewed ships that make up the Military Sealift Command. These ships replenish U.S. Navy ships, conduct specialized missions, strategically preposition combat cargo at sea and around the world and move military cargo and supplies used by deployed U.S. forces.

I was taken to a room off of the bridge and met Captain Frank Ballard. In his late fifties with silver hair and kind eyes, he had a pleasant manner. We shook hands, and after the usual pleasantries, he asked me if I'd like to see a map detailing what had happened during the day once they got the call to come to my aid. Yes! Hopefully, this would answer all of the questions I had regarding my rescue.

USNS Meteor, Pearl Harbor

He walked me over to a large table. Laid out was a map of our current location of the Pacific Ocean.

"Right where this 'x' is, is where you went down. In the nine and a half hours that you were in the raft, you drifted eleven miles. You were a little over 500 miles from the Hawaiian Islands."

I could see lots of markings and lines on the map, some dots, some 'x's, some lines were dashed, others were solid. But Captain Ballard was patient in making sense out of it all.

He continued. "We were about here," and he pointed to a circle, "when we got the call that you were in a four-man life raft and needed assistance. We were the closest ship."

I explained to him that the last bit of information I had received was that they were going to dispatch a destroyer out of Pearl Harbor to come get me. Did he know if they had done that?

"Even though the call for help was made a couple of hours before you went down, they would not have sent the destroyer until they had confirmation that you had survived the ditching," he explained.

I was glad that aid hadn't been wasted in the efforts to find me. Hmm. I wondered if I was going to get a bill from the government for all of this.

He went on. "And this is where it got confusing," as his index finger circled an area on the chart. "We were talking to a couple of rescue planes that were giving us directions to find you. They kept asking us if we saw the flares that were being dropped, and we did, but they were way off in the distance. I had every single man on board up on deck searching with binoculars for you. No matter how hard we tried, we could not see you, even though the planes were telling us that we were, basically, right on top of you. We were very disappointed that it was not us that eventually found you."

I could tell from the sound of his voice that he was being sincere.

"Then, we heard that someone had picked you up and you were safe. We got clarification of the rescue ship's exact location, and when we compared it to what we had been given, we were twenty miles south. We had been given the wrong coordinates. So, with all of the confusion of planes coming and going out of Hilo and Honolulu, they were looking at the Soviet ship, but talking to us, confusing their ship as our ship."

"So, why wasn't someone talking to the Soviets? Isn't there a common emergency frequency for that sort of thing?" I asked.

He explained that airplanes use VHF, Very High Frequency, frequencies when talking to one another and to air traffic control. The maritime, ship to ship, radios use VHF-FM frequencies, so it may have been difficult for the Soviet ship to have heard any radio transmissions originating from aircraft.

"I'm sure that they were seeing the flares that were being dropped, knew that someone was in trouble, and just started following them. They probably didn't know *what* they were looking for. You were very lucky. And frankly, I don't know how we were able to eventually find a way to communicate with them. Their radio operator was the only one that spoke English, and we have one man on board that speaks a little Russian. But it all worked out and you are heading home."

He asked me if there was anything special that I needed, besides some dry clothes. I asked him if there was a way that I could call my parents and let them know that I was okay. He assured me that I could do that right away.

He called for the chief engineer to escort me below to the radio room where I could get a call placed to my family. Just as we were leaving, he said, "Breakfast is at seven. Have them seat you at my table." I immediately realized that this was not a request, but an order, albeit a very polite one. I felt what it must be like to be in the military.

On the way to the radio room, the steward handed me a khaki jumpsuit, a bar of soap, a toothbrush, toothpaste, and a comb.

We arrived in the small, cramped radio room and the chief engineer was able to patch a phone call back to California for me. My mom answered after the second ring.

"Hi Mom. A funny thing happened on the way to Hawaii."

"IT'S HEIDI! DOUG, GET ON THE PHONE. IT'S HEIDI!"

Within seconds, my father was on the extension. Between the two of them, they must have asked if I was alright about a dozen times before they would take my word that I was fine. I don't really remember the rest of the conversation. I know that I wasn't up to hashing over all of the details with them. They asked me questions that I couldn't answer, like 'When are you coming home?' I didn't know what was going to happen at that point going forward. All I knew was that I was headed for Honolulu, and I'd call them when I had more details.

We ended the call, and I assumed that the chief would escort me to my quarters. It was almost three in the morning, and I could barely keep my eyes open. I hadn't slept onboard the Soviet ship, so by now I couldn't even remember the last time I had slept. However, the chief was a talkative sort. I think he was happy to have a captive audience in his workspace, of which he was very proud. I didn't want to be rude, so I just listened to him telling me about his family, his job, and his career. I tried not to ask him any questions which might extend the conversation. After about 30 minutes, he finally showed me to my quarters.

The room was about half the size of the one onboard the Soviet ship. There was a bunkbed against the wall, a desk and chair, and a small adjacent bathroom with a wall sink, toilet, and in the corner, a small shower with a shower curtain. I was too tired to even brush my teeth. All I could think of was to climb under the blanket.

Just as I was about to undress, there was a soft tap at the door. It was the steward.

"Here are some fresh towels for you."

As I took them with my thanks, I asked him if he could give me a wakeup call at 6:30 so I would not be late for breakfast with the captain. He promised that he would.

As I slid beneath the covers of the bottom bunk, I found it hard to fully relax. I knew I was safe, at last, but I couldn't shut my mind off of all that had happened in the last 24 hours. Slowly, I started to 'let go' and pray that sleep would come. But then I noticed and felt something strange. About every 45 seconds I would feel a strange rumbling that would last about three to four seconds, and then it would stop. This went on for a few minutes. 'Oh great!' I thought. 'Did they put me directly over the engine room? Was this going to go on all night, not that there was much 'night' left?'

Then I realized. It wasn't coming from the engine room; it was me shuddering.

Twenty-Six

Regrets

Having always been a light sleeper, I did not need a wakeup call, after all. I awoke around 6:15 am, not knowing where I was for at least thirty seconds, which seemed an eternity. My whole body was sore, and it was difficult for me to get out of the bunk and stand on my feet. Suddenly, everything came rushing back.

The tiny shower felt wonderful on my aching muscles. I even managed to wash my hair within the confines of the small space. I noticed that the large bruise on my right upper arm was warm to the touch, and firmer that the surrounding tissue. It was deep purple, almost black in color. 'Should I be concerned?' I thought. It seemed a minor concern at the time. But my thoughts were interrupted by the knock at the door. It was the Steward telling me that it was 6:30. I thanked him and said that I would be on time for breakfast with the captain.

As I stared at my puffy, sleep-deprived face, with only a toothbrush and comb for toiletries, I was relieved, in a way, that I had no choice in the matter to make myself look more presentable. I was now the epitome of the 'low maintenance woman.' In all honesty, it was freeing. I towel dried my wet hair as best I could, ran the comb through it, brushed my teeth, and I was ready to face the day.

I stepped outside my quarters, and into the long gray corridor. Now, which way was the 'mess'? Within a minute, I encountered a seaman, who seemed surprised to see me. I asked him to point me in the direction of the Mess, and he gave me excellent instructions. Thankfully, it wasn't that far away. As I made my way towards my destination, I ran into a couple of other seamen. They smiled, but did not speak to me.

I entered the Mess, assuming that I would be the first one there, as it only took me ten minutes to get ready after the Steward knocked on my door. But there I found a large round table, a crisp white tablecloth in place, where six of the officers were already seated, one last open chair for me. They all stood when I approached. I had a flashback to the dinner in Pago Pago and the Australian officers who had invited me to join them. They stood for me, as well. Will there be a gift of a bottle of rum or port at the end of this meal, too? It was I that should be handing out gifts.

Captain Ballard made the introductions of his chief officers. I apologized for my appearance, but they assured me that since I should be dead right now, I looked pretty damn good. We all laughed.

I was absolutely starving! I realized that I hadn't really eaten anything for over two days. The minute I got on board a ship, the nausea ceased, so I knew that the reason for my upset stomach was because of the ingested sea water, and not a case of seasickness. Great! Bring on the food. I felt confident that I would be able to keep it down.

The chief steward addressed me first and took my order. In homage to my Soviet hosts, I ordered fried eggs, bacon, and toast. And coffee! And then the questions started, the first being, "What the HELL were you doing out there!" So, I explained the details of my occupation and the ferry company I flew for, that this was the tenth over-water delivery I had done, and it wasn't some kind of frivolous whim on my part. They listened intently. (My food was getting cold.) When I described in detail how we navigated, communicated, and prepared the planes for flight, they seemed to agree that maybe I knew what I was doing. They still thought I was crazy for doing these types of flights, but they respected the process.

I decided that if I wanted to get any sustenance, I had better start asking some questions of them. They told me that we were headed for Pearl Harbor, and that we would arrive around 6:00 am the following morning. I told them that I was a huge World War II enthusiast, and Captain Ballard invited me to join him on the bridge the following morning to get a good view of our entrance into the harbor.

As breakfast was dying down, Captain Ballard told me that I could have free run of the ship, and to ask if I needed an escort. Not wanting to put them to any more trouble than I had already, I asked him if there was a quiet space where I could write down a sort of 'diary' of what had happened in the previous three days, so I would not forget in future years. The First Mate showed me to a lounge, just off of the Mess, and found some paper and a pen for me to use. I got to writing.

When I needed a break, I considered taking a walk around the ship, but from the reaction I had received from some of the seamen I had encountered earlier, I assumed that maybe the effort to rescue me had been an unwelcome distraction, so I did not want to intrude any further. Much later, I discovered that the captain had told the crew to give me a 'wide berth' and not to bother me unless I approached them first. Maybe he assumed that I would be traumatized by the ditching experience. I know that if I had known that the crew had been given those instructions, I would have made the effort to meet each and every one of those men and shake each and every hand. Opportunity lost.

I didn't need to worry about getting a 'writer's cramp' in my hand. It seemed that during the day, and into the afternoon, I was paged up to the bridge on several occasions. The ship was receiving multiple phone calls from the press and media, all wanting an interview. It seems that getting rescued in the middle of the night by a Soviet refrigeration vessel during the Cold War was news.

I accepted the first two requests to speak to reporters upon arrival at Pearl. I assumed that I would meet with them somewhere off base. But they made it clear that they wanted to come aboard to talk to me. This was a different story altogether.

"Captain Ballard, this is *your* ship. I will do whatever you think is best for your ship and crew."

The Captain came to the conclusion that it would be much more organized and controlled to have a press conference in his quarters the following morning. He was extremely gracious, and after some consideration, had made a smart decision. I would have been mortified if I gave inaccurate information about the Meteor and the crew's efforts to rescue me.

In all, there must have been six to seven times when my presence was requested on the bridge to talk to newspaper reporters and television news stations. When the CBS affiliate phoned, they asked me if there was anything I needed that they could bring to the ship for me. Did I need a hotel? Clothes? I declined their offer as I assumed I would be able to take care of all of that once we docked. An hour later, it hit me. 'Why hadn't I told them that I would like to meet up with Tom Selleck from the show *Magnum, P.I.*?!' I had a terrible crush on him and watched his show religiously. I would probably never have another opportunity like that again. Oh well. Another opportunity lost.

I managed to take a short nap before dinner. I met with the same group of officers that evening, and it was much more relaxed, although they had a new round of questions for me. But this time I interspersed my answers with questions of my own. This time, the food stayed semi-warm.

After dinner, we all went into the lounge and watched the movie, *The Right Stuff*, about the development of the Mercury space program and the astronauts involved. I had seen the movie when it had been released the year before, but I enjoyed watching it a second time, even though I found it nearly impossible to keep my eyes open.

I didn't waste much time falling asleep. The trembling had stopped, my soreness was easing a bit after a hot shower, my stomach had managed to keep all of my meals contained, and I'd be on dry land in a few hours.

But soon after my eyelids closed, I found myself thinking, *DAMN! I probably could have met Tom Selleck!*

Twenty-Seven

Pearl Harbor
August 14, 1984

My subconscious alarm went off somewhere around 5:15 the following morning. I did not want to be late for the arrival into Pearl Harbor. Once again, I appreciated that I did not have to waste time on wardrobe, hair, and makeup. The only adornment I wore was the black plastic whistle on the twine string around my neck. I had not taken it off since being in the raft.

I made my way up to the lounge, where I had spent so much time the previous day, and was grateful to find a self-serve coffee setup. I could tell that there were crew around by the soft noises coming from the deck, but I did not see anyone. I knew my way up to the bridge, as I must have made a dozen trips there during my writing session.

When I got to a spot in the railing on the starboard side of the ship, just outside of the entrance to the bridge, I stood in amazement at the sight. My friend, the moon, still cast its ethereal light over the water, making it shimmer in sparkles of silver. On the horizon was a mass of blackness; the hills to the north of Waikiki. They offered their own rendering of beauty; tiny bright dots of lights from the homes of the people who were so fortunate to live in such an extraordinary place. And there, just at the water's edge was the familiar rotating beacon of white-green strobe lights flashing to identify the Honolulu International Airport. With each passing minute,

I could discern that the sun would be making its appearance within the next half hour.

I was caught up in the peacefulness of the moment, when Captain Ballard appeared and wished me a good morning. He invited me into the bridge and showed me a map of the entrance we would make into the harbor.

Pearl Harbor only has one channel for entry and exit. It is at the southern end of the harbor, immediately to the west of the airport. Shortly after entering the channel, it forks into a 'Y,' the majority of the military complex towards the right of the fork. Once in this channel, Ford Island is off the port side, with most of the docking facilities on the starboard. Our docking location would be just shy of the location where the Navy battleship, the USS Arizona, was sunk by the Japanese during their attack on Pearl Harbor on December 7, 1941.

We walked out onto the starboard 'flybridge,' an open deck area off of the bridge that offers unobstructed views of the fore, aft, and side of the ship. The sky was lightening, but the sun had not risen yet. We looked to the north, and Captain Ballard pointed towards a mountain ridge that ran north-south on the western side of Oahu.

"See that pass to the east of the mountains?"

"Yes, sir" I said.

"The Japanese made their first wave of attacks flying through that pass from the north, and then swinging to the west of the harbor. They separated their torpedo planes into three groups, one hitting us from the northwest, one from the west, and one from the south. A fourth group made up of bombers hit us from the southwest. Their second wave, about an hour later, also came from the north, but flew along the east side of the island, over the water, to hit us with High Level bombers from the south, east and northeast." He spoke as if he had seen it with his own eyes. Maybe he had a family member that had been in the war.

Years before, I had studied the attack on Pearl Harbor, so I was familiar with the tactics. And during a Honolulu layover during one of my previous ferry flights, I had the opportunity to tour the USS Bowfin, a submarine used during the war. But seeing the harbor from this vantage point was more than most tourists would ever see. I soaked it all in and was grateful that Captain Ballard was taking time out of a very busy morning to share his knowledge with me. We kept our conversation to a minimum, almost like we were at a church service.

I left him to his duties as we entered the channel. I tried to imagine what it must have been like to have been a sailor on the morning of December 7, 1941, and to live through the terror of those few hours. It seemed like the seamen on deck appreciated the solemnity of the history of this harbor as well.

Captain Ballard suggested that we meet for breakfast once docking was complete. I looked forward to seeing the officers once again so I could express my deep appreciation for all that they and their crew had done for me. I had enough time to freshen up a bit, pack my 'belongings,' a toothbrush and comb, and my precious gifts from the Soviets. I stripped the bunk and collected my used towels, so the room would be easy to clean after my departure.

The usual group of officers were there to greet me in the mess, and just as we were sitting down to some coffee, Earl walked in, a lei of carnations in his hand. In the back of my mind, I suspected that he might be in Honolulu waiting for my arrival, but part of me thought that he might have continued the ferry flight on to New Zealand as the customers were always anxious to get their hands on the airplanes.

Earl greeted me by placing the lei of flowers around my neck, and giving me a hug. I introduced Earl to Captain Ballard, and the captain introduced Earl to the rest of the officers. A place setting was put down on the table for Earl to join us.

The next hour was spent in a conversation mostly about Transair, and Earl's experiences flying over water. I was actually able to finish a meal while the food remained hot, so I didn't mind Earl being the center of attention. But then it was time to go to

Captain Ballard's quarters for the press conference.

I was shocked. There must have been 20 to 25 people packed into the small office adjoining Captain Ballard's personal quarters. There were press reporters, television reporters, cameramen, and still photographers. More leis were placed around my neck, which made me happy. Maybe the flowers would distract them from seeing how fatigued and shabby I looked.

And then the questions started. It was like something out of a movie. I could barely finish answering one question, when another would be asked. Now I got an understanding why some newspaper articles were not as accurate as they should have been. But I had my own agenda. I wanted to make sure that I expressed to all present how wonderful the Soviets had been, to explain that they were not obligated to participate in my rescue, that they could have abandoned the search at any time. And I wanted to give credit to the P-3 units and the Coast Guard Search and Rescue Command C-130s, the men and women of VP-91, the P-3 unit known as the 'Stingers,' for intercepting me at the very beginning, and also to the Military Sealift Command, with Captain Frank Ballard, for bringing me 'home.' I did not want all those associated with my rescue to go unrecognized. And, of course, I mentioned how important it was to have Earl as my wingman.

Press conference, Capt. Ballard's quarters

As the press conference was breaking up, someone from the NBC affiliate offered to pay for hotel accommodations for me. In return, I would agree to appear on the television program, *The Today Show*, via satellite. I accepted their offer, and when asked where I would like to stay, Earl suggested a hotel near Waikiki that would be appropriate. This caught me off-guard a bit, but I didn't want to press the point. NBC told me I could choose any hotel, and I had always been curious what that famous pale pink hotel on the beach would be like. But based upon the sleeping accommodations I had experienced the last few days, any hotel with a full-size tub and shower, and a normal-sized bed would have fit the bill.

Earl, Heidi, Capt. Frank Ballard

It was finally time to leave. This was bittersweet. I had bonded with these people, and I was sorry to say goodbye. Captain

Ballard escorted Earl and me off the ship, and someone took a group picture, the Meteor in the background. I gave Captain Ballard a big hug and kissed his cheek. I know I had tears in my eyes. I watched him as he climbed the gangplank and as Earl and I started walking towards his rental car I remembered something.

"My RAFT!"

The day before, one of the officers had told me that one of the Soviets had lowered my bundled-up raft down into the American launch and it was transferred onto the ship. I couldn't leave without getting my raft!

I felt a bit foolish going back onboard the Meteor. We had already said our goodbyes. But fortunately, I quickly found a seaman who knew exactly where my raft had been kept, and he brought it to me.

Next step? Back to reality.

Twenty-Eight

Loose Ends

"So, where to?" I asked Earl as we drove off.

"Well, the FAA wants to talk to you to so they can file a report, and the Coast Guard and Navy would each like to do a debriefing with you by phone. So, let's get those out of the way before getting you to the hotel."

A pilot never wants to hear those words, "The FAA would like to talk to you," but I understood the necessity. I wanted to talk to them while everything was fresh in my mind. And I was actually looking forward to talking to the Navy and Coast Guard to help fill in the blanks I still had regarding their procedures for search and rescue.

"But first, we have to make one stop," Earl said.

A few minutes later we found ourselves sharing a bottle of champagne at the historic Monkey Bar, a famous tavern popular with servicemen during World War II. Behind the bar was a glassed off area which encompassed an area for several spider monkeys to inhabit.

I was still pretty tired from the previous few days, and so it didn't take much alcohol to relax me. And it felt good to celebrate the successful outcome of my ordeal. Earl, having been present during the press conference, was up to speed on what transpired after he had to leave me at the ditching site, but he had some questions for me, none the less. It was his opinion that the reason for the engine quitting was caused by a failure of the oil pump. I wasn't sure about this. If the pump had failed, wouldn't there have been an instantaneous loss of pressure? I explained to him the loss of pressure was gradual. But then, I'm not a mechanic, so there was the possibility that he was correct. On later conjecture, on my part, maybe there was some concern that the company might be liable for the engine running out of oil. On some airplanes that we ferried, we had a way of being able to add oil to the engine from the cockpit while in flight. It's my opinion that had we installed this system, the engine might not have quit. Of course, that is nearly impossible to prove.

He also asked me several times as to why I was not able to get any of my extra survival supplies out of the aircraft. I explained to him several times that it had taken every bit of energy I had to get into the raft successfully, I had to cut the only tether I had connecting me to the raft, I was not a strong swimmer, by any means, and that I did not know how fast the plane would be going down. What I didn't know at the time, was that my employee benefit of an insurance policy covering the loss of my equipment had been canceled a few months before, as a cost-cutting measure, so I was uninsured. It was going to be my loss.

We made some plans for the rest of the day. We would file my report with the FAA, have the debriefings with the Coast Guard and Navy, and then check into my hotel. Earl had been staying at our usual layover hotel which was near the airport. Then Earl would take me to a shopping mall so I could get some clothes and other necessities. That evening, he would drive me to the television studio.

We drove to the local FAA office, and met a very nice man who walked me through the questions for the report. He also recorded the interview. At the end of the session, he felt confident that there was no pilot error, but for me to expect a call from the NTSB, the National Transportation Safety Board. They would want more details. I could tell that he was more interested in my story, than the 'nuts and bolts' questions on the government form. When we were done, he told us that we could use his conference room to have the phone debriefings with the Coast Guard and Navy.

The formats for the discussions with both agencies were basically the same. They explained that there are so few successful rescues at sea, they needed to know what worked, and what didn't. What could they do better in the future?

After telling them how grateful I was for all of their efforts, and what a comfort it had been to see the various planes circling overhead, I told them that it would have been helpful to me to have an explanation of what I could expect in the hours following the ditching; what type of supplies, if any, would be dropped to me, how long could I expect to be out there, how would they keep track of my position, and if they discerned that I was really hurt, would someone have gotten into the water with me, or would I have been left alone?

On their part, they were very interested in why I had decided not to stall the airplane, and instead 'flew' the airplane to the water. But mostly, they wanted to know why I had stayed in my raft after the larger raft and supplies had been dropped to me. After a debriefing with the pilots of the rescue planes who witnessed the aftermath of the drop, they were sure that I would have attempted to swim to the supplies, just as anyone else would have, but they knew that I never would have made it. They were glad to hear my explanation of why I stayed put. I finished by expressing again how much it meant to me that everyone involved gave one hundred percent.

The debriefings took about an hour and a half to complete, longer than we had anticipated. It didn't make sense to go to the hotel first. I had nothing to unpack, and Earl promised me that he would take care of my raft for me. So, it was off to the mall.

Earl dropped me off at the Ala Moana shopping mall, and told me that he would meet me at a pizza parlor there in about two hours for a late lunch. He gave me an advance of $200, as I had no money or credit cards.

Why is it that when you do not need clothing, you run

across outfits that you really like, but when you really need something, they're impossible to find? That was my case. I felt rushed because I did not want to keep Earl waiting. The image popped into my mind of movie scenes where you see men sitting in the women's clothing section of a store, bored out of their minds, looking at their watches, while their girlfriends or wives take their time trying on outfits.

I eventually found a navy-blue cotton skirt, a belt, a light blue button down short-sleeved shirt, some underwear, and casual shoes. I didn't need any jewelry; I had my whistle for a necklace. I bought a few items of makeup, a hairbrush, curling iron, and some toiletries. The hotel would provide shampoo and soap. It wasn't the most stylish ensemble, but it would have to do.

I met Earl for some pizza, and then we made our way to my hotel. I don't recall the name of the hotel, but it was along the Waikiki strip, but across the street from the water. Earl came with me while I checked in. A stack of messages was given to me by the front desk clerk. Earl asked if he could make a couple of phone calls from my room. Remember, this was before cell phones.

The phone was already ringing as we walked into my room. I sat on the edge of one of the twin beds, next to the nightstand, and started answering phone calls. They were mostly from various news agencies from around the country. As soon as I would hang up, another call would announce itself within seconds. A 'turf war' developed between CBS, ABC and NBC. They all wanted to interview me for their morning shows on the East Coast. I had already promised NBC that I would do their show, but ABC pressed hard for me to be on their show instead. Eventually, they had to back down, as the only time slot they had available conflicted with the time NBC wanted me. But I was able to agree to be on CBS Morning News with Bill Kurtis after my interview with NBC and Bryant Gumbel.

With the time change between Hawaii and the East Coast, I would need to be at the NBC affiliate studio in Honolulu before midnight. It was already three in the afternoon. And there was still a stack of messages to get through, besides wanting to call home. The incoming calls were relentless in their frequency. I finally had to put a stop to it. I called the front desk and said, "Unless it is family, please hold my calls." This was a phrase I never imagined myself saying. Important business moguls and Hollywood celebrities say that kind of stuff. Not someone like me!

It was late enough in the day that by the time Earl was to drive back to his hotel and then back again, he would only have a few hours before we would have to leave for the studio. Always trying to be aware of the needs of others, I offered Earl the use of one of the two beds in my room to take a nap. I expected him to thank me, but turn me down. So, it came as a surprise when he agreed. He said that he hadn't gotten much sleep in the past few days either. And frankly, the Pacific Marina Hotel, where we usually stayed, left something to be desired.

It was then that I realized that I had not purchased any sleep wear. So, I found a new use for the khaki jumpsuit that the Meteor crew had given me. Unfortunately, it was a bit short in the torso, so it was not the most comfortable set of 'pajamas' I had ever worn. I had a hard time sleeping. I had never been on national television before. I was worried that I might make a fool out of myself, but eventually I managed to doze off.

I had left a wakeup call with the front desk so I would not oversleep. When the phone rang, they informed me that NBC had sent a car for me to take me to the studio, and would be waiting downstairs for me. I could tell from Earl's voice that he was still very tired, so I told him to stay put, and I would go to the studios alone. After all, he had a lot of flying ahead of him.

Twenty-Nine

Take the Shot!

I arrived at the NBC studio for my interview with Bryant Gumbel. They placed me on a tall chair, a tv camera about five feet away, pointed directly at me, and I was wired with an earphone so I could hear New York, but I would not be able to see them. They had arranged to have my parents, Doug, and Gloria, in a studio in San Francisco at the same time.

I found it interesting to hear the background conversations going on during the commercial breaks. I could tell from Mr. Gumbel's raised voice that he was not happy with the lighting crew. Was he going to be this abrupt when talking to me? I was expecting him to take a moment and let me know how the interview would proceed; what questions he would be asking me, but he did not speak to me until the interview started. A crewman standing in the shadows next to the tv camera in front of me waved that I would be 'on' in just a few seconds. My heart began to pound. Bryant Gumbel spoke.

"Imagine yourself flying across the Pacific Ocean, alone. It's the dead of night. You're in a howling storm and your oil pressure drops. Your engine overheats. You're forced to crash land into a heaving sea. Then, after ditching the plane you're forced to wrestle the ocean in a bucking life raft. No food, no water, only one flare. This morning, we get to meet a woman who went through all this just three nights ago. Her name is Heidi Porch."

My mind was reeling. As he spoke, I thought, *My god! Did someone else ditch?*

It wasn't until I heard him say my name that I realized he was talking about me, but the facts were all wrong. I wasn't alone. It was two in the afternoon, the weather was near perfect, the sea was almost calm, and the raft wasn't a problem until late at night. AND, most pilots take offense at the word, 'Crash.' Mine was a 'ditching,' or a 'forced landing.' The word crash implies a lack of pilot control. Okay, I thought…here we go.

His first question caught me off guard, as well.

"Heidi, do you consider yourself lucky to be alive? Are you surprised you were able to survive your ordeal?"

How was I supposed to answer that? Of course luck was involved, but it also took the efforts of a whole helluva lot of people doing their jobs, and I was grateful. I felt that if I told him I was surprised at my survival, it would indicate that I was just 'along for the ride,' and had no input into increasing the odds that I would make it.

"You don't look any worse for wear from this. Have you any injuries from the experience?"

Show 'em, Heidi, show 'em! I thought. Where were my 'better angels' when I needed them to stop me from doing something so embarrassing? To this day, I just shake my head at the thought of what I did.

I extended my arm, pulled up my sleeve, and proudly displayed the bruise on my right arm, now a disgusting shade of yellow, green, and purple. Well, I guess it could have been worse. The bruise could have been on my butt.

Bryant Gumbel pivoted to my parents. In a way, I felt sorry for Mr. Gumbel. My father had the habit of speaking very slowly, and incorporating a lot of 'Uhhs, and Umms.' I could tell that it was difficult for Mr. Gumbel to keep the pace of the interview going.

The interview proceeded with questions about how the Russians treated me, and my mother, being a mother, said that she wanted to make sure that I would get a good night's sleep before flying again. And then the big question came.

To my parents, "Would you like to see her move into a different line of work, one that perhaps doesn't have so many risks attended to it?"

My father knew as much as I did that here was a golden opportunity.

"Well, we'd like to see her achieve her heart's desire and that's to fly for an airline."

The wheels inside my head were at full speed. *This is your chance, Heidi! National TV. TAKE THE SHOT!*

"Heidi, any chance you are going to move out of this profession?"

This was it.

In as upbeat of a voice as I could manage, I responded, "Like my father said, since age seven I've wanted to fly for the airlines. Actually, I blame the whole ordeal on them. If they'd have hired me like I wanted them to I wouldn't have been in that situation." And then I interrupted Mr. Gumbel's laughter by continuing.

"Okay, if any airlines are listening, I'm available!"

Thirty

Night and Day

Next was the CBS interview with Bill Kurtis. The set up was the same; I had an earpiece where I could hear the interviewer, but could not see him. I had about twenty minutes before my segment began. During a commercial break, I was startled to hear Mr. Kurtis say hello to me.

"Hello, Heidi. This is Bill. I'm sure you had quite the experience and I can't wait to talk to you about it. I will be asking you the same type of questions that you have probably been answering for the past few days. But is there anything that you would like to say that you haven't had the opportunity to talk about yet?"

I was taken aback at his kindness and sincerity. His easy-going manner helped me relax during the interview and in viewing it afterwards it was apparent that I was having a good time in talking to him. His first question to me was whether I had been injured in the ditching. This time, my better angels were at their posts, and I kept my bruise to myself.

With my media obligations fulfilled for the night, I could finally get back to the hotel for a few hours of sleep. However, I had more duties for the morning. Apparently, the reason Earl had suggested that I stay at this particular hotel was because the Kiwanis would meet there for their monthly meetings. Earl was a member, and had told them that I would speak about my experiences at their gathering, which happened to be later that morning.

It was the first time I had ever spoken to a group that large; there were probably around 40 guests. Fortunately, I was still tired enough that I didn't have the energy to be nervous. What helped was that in looking at their faces, I could tell that they were genuinely interested in my story, so that eased my nerves.

After the meeting, it was time for Earl to be on his way with the aircraft delivery. The client in New Zealand had been patient, but business was business. He needed the airplane. We said our goodbyes, I thanked him for all of his help, and told him I'd see him after he got back from New Zealand to tie up loose ends.

I was hoping for some 'down time' on my own, but the phone in my hotel room was just as busy as it had been the day before. Part of me wanted to stay a couple of days, just to relax. During ferry deliveries, we would only spend a few hours at each layover, just enough time to eat and sleep, before continuing on to our next island stop. It would be a nice change to sit by the water, and reflect on all that had happened. But I knew that my family was anxious to have me back home.

Earl had made arrangements for me to take a Pan Am flight home to San Francisco that very evening. He traded in the one-way coach ticket from New Zealand to San Francisco that wouldn't be needed, for a one-way first-class ticket. I planned on getting out to the airport a bit early so I could relax in the airline lounge for a glass of wine before the flight boarded.

As I entered the lounge, I received strange looks from some of the patrons, especially from a woman in stylish clothes. Gone are the days when people dress up to fly commercially. She was with the rest of her family. My carry on luggage consisted of one paper shopping bag. I'm sure they thought that I had entered the lounge under false pretenses, but no one challenged me.

I sipped my glass of wine and nibbled on some cheese and crackers. It was nice to be alone and in a 'normal' setting, where questions weren't being lobbed at me every few seconds. And then it was time to board.

Pan Am flew 747's between Hawaii and the mainland. It was the 'classic' 747, with the spiral staircase leading to the upstairs deck. My seat was on the main deck in one of the middle two seats that had aisles on either side. We would be flying all night, and arriving at San Francisco at sunrise, so I didn't mind not having a window seat. But who should I end up sitting next to? My seat mate would be the woman from the passenger lounge who had shown such disdain and condescension towards me. I smushed my 'suitcase' into the overhead compartment, and took my seat next to her.

Not wanting to be rude, I said, "Good evening."

A sweeping glance from her, but no response. I took the hint. I would leave her be for the duration of the flight.

I was hoping that I might recognize one of the flight attendants, as I frequented Pan Am so often on my flights home from Australia, but none of them seemed familiar. The service, however, was the usual top-notch performance, even if Homer wasn't perched on top of my seat.

I managed to sleep for a few hours, but was wide awake before we started the descent into San Francisco. The rest of the passengers were getting ready for our arrival, as well. My seat mate visited the lavatory and returned freshly coiffed and perfumed. I didn't feel like digging into the bottom of my paper bag to retrieve my hairbrush, so I went to the restroom and splashed some water on my face.

As I sat down again, she looked up at me, and I thought I'd try one more time.

"Do you live here in San Francisco, or are you continuing on?"

"Yes."

Yes, what? I thought. I wasn't going to press the point.

We taxied into the gate, and my 'friend' and her family made a beeline for the door. I was about four people behind them. As we were funneled into the long jet bridge, we were hit by a collection of blinding lights and crowd noises coming from the end of the jet bridge, in the gate area ahead.

"Ooh!" my 'friend' exclaimed. "There must have been someone famous on our flight! Let's wait to see who it is!"

Above their heads, I could see the smiling faces of my mother, my father, my sisters, Allison and Lisa, my aunt, our family friends, Joe and Denise, and my best friend, Robin. The second I emerged from the jet bridge, I was surrounded by the press and television crews, their cameras and lights pointed at me, and microphones jutting towards my face. I spent the next few minutes hugging my family and friends to the tune of many greetings welcoming me home. I think I even got a few backslaps from some of the news people.

I managed to take a look at my seat mate standing off to the side next to her husband. I could read the expression of puzzlement on her face, her mouth open. She was probably thinking, *Who the hell is this person? Maybe I should have spoken to her.*

Thirty-One

One Good Turn

The madness continued once I got home. Newspapers and the local television stations were calling for interviews. I tried to accommodate as many as I could, but it was beginning to wear on me. I was receiving newspaper clippings from around the country from friends and relations. Someone even sent me a full-size copy of a magazine, the size of the old 'LIFE' magazine. But this one was titled, "Soviet Life." Inside was a small article describing my rescue, from the viewpoint of the Soviets. I couldn't help but laugh at all of the inconsistencies in their story.

Soviet Life magazine

Rescue Came in the Nick of Time

☐ American sportswoman Ann Porch was making a flight from the United States to Australia with a stopover on the Pacific Islands for rest and refueling. The weather wasn't very good—a typhoon was forecast for the vicinity—but Porch calculated that she would be able to make her first landing before it got too bad. Suddenly, hundreds of miles from land, the plane's engine began to sputter, and the craft began to lose altitude. It wasn't too long before the engine died altogether.

Porch had barely enough time to radio an SOS signal and give her approximate coordinates before the plane plunged into the ocean. Fortunately, she managed to get out of the craft and climb onto a rubber raft. The weather conditions continued to worsen.

The Soviet refrigerator ship the *Ussuriiskaya Taiga* was en route to Vladivostok when it saw a U.S. Coast Guard plane signaling overhead. From the plane's maneuvers the captain understood that it wanted the vessel to follow it. It was clear that someone was in trouble and the Soviet ship's help was needed in the rescue.

Porch was unconscious when she was lifted aboard the Soviet vessel. The ship's doctor examined her and found her body temperature dangerously low, but with treatment she soon recovered.

Porch was later transferred to an American naval vessel and taken to Hawaii. The Hawaiian authorities radioed their appreciation.

Article about the rescue appearing in Soviet Life magazine.

Out of the thirty to forty clippings I received, perhaps two or three were accurate. Since then, it has made me question the accuracy of what I read in print or watch on television. It has forced me to seek out several sources to get an accurate account, which isn't a bad thing.

About four days after getting home I received a call.

"Hello, Heidi? You don't know me, but do you remember hearing a voice over the radio before you ditched saying, 'ALRIGHT, HEIDI'?"

It took me a few moments, and then it came back.

"Yes! I do! Was that you?"

"No, that was our Captain, Bob Stevenson. I was the First Officer. We were flying overhead, but the whole crew and most of the stewardesses were in the cockpit listening in on your situation. We thought that the P-3 was going to leave you before the Coast Guard got to you, and we were all screaming, 'DON'T LET THEM GO! MAKE THEM STAY! When you told them that you wanted them to stick around, Bob couldn't help himself, and he yelled 'Alright, Heidi!'"

I laughed.

"Listen," he said. "Captain Stevenson is retiring. He is one of our most beloved pilots at American. We are throwing him a surprise retirement party, and I know he would love to meet you. Would you consider coming? You know, when we got to Honolulu, he was the first person off of the plane, on the phone to the Coast Guard, to make sure everything was being done to get you picked up."

It only took me two seconds to think about it.

"Absolutely! I'd love to meet him, and all of you."

Fortunately, most of them lived in the Bay Area, so it was an easy drive to where the party would be held.

That weekend I arrived at the party about an hour before the guest of honor would arrive. The yard was decorated in a Hawaiian theme, and they greeted me with a lei to wear. 'I could get used to this,' I thought.

Introduction to Capt. Bob Stevenson, First Officer and
Purser (in back)

I met the First Officer, who had tracked me down in order to invite me to the party, the Flight Engineer, the Purser, and several of the Flight Attendants from the flight on August 12th. There were many others in attendance, mostly flight crews that had flown with Captain Stevenson over the years, and many family members. I loved listening to their stories about Bob. He sounded like the perfect airline Captain; professional, knowledgeable, supportive, kind and encouraging. I couldn't wait to meet him. But mostly, I was hoping that one day, I would be able to fly as a First Officer for a captain as wonderful as Captain Stevenson.

They had me hide around the back side of the house until Bob made his appearance. I think I was more nervous waiting to meet him, as I was during any of the interviews I had been giving. It was only a few minutes before I heard everyone yell, "Surprise!"

"Bob… Captain Stevenson, there is someone we'd like you to meet."

Capt. Bob Stevenson and Heidi

That was my cue. I walked around the corner of the house, and Bob stood there, a semi-circle of his friends and family behind him.

He looked at me while I approached, a blank look on his face. *Do I know this girl? Who is she? Oh my God, is this some illegitimate daughter that I didn't know I had?!* The blank look on his face morphed into one of *Get me out of here.*

"Hello, Captain Stevenson. I'm Heidi Porch. The one from the life raft."

A glorious smile slowly broke across his face. He held my arms, and then wrapped his arms around me in one of the warmest hugs I've ever had. We bonded instantly.

Some good things do come from bad.

Thirty-Two

Endings

It took a couple of weeks, but life slowly began to return to normal. The media moved on to other news stories, and I began to make plans for how I would continue working at Transair. I had lost most, if not all, of my survival equipment in the ditching. I knew that I wanted to get back in the air as soon as possible, but it would be very expensive for me to replace the items I had lost.

I was visiting with my friend, Ernie Hummel. We had made plans for one of our 'champagne dates' sitting on our favorite log at the glider port, sipping the wine out of paper cups. It was the first time that I had a chance to spend some time alone with him since I had returned. As usual, I wanted his advice on what I should do next.

"You know, Heidi," he calmly said. "Whenever you would go on one of these ferry flights, your parents would not sleep all night until they knew you had made it to Hawaii. They hated it. But they never told you. They know how important your flying is to you."

That's all I needed to hear. I decided right then that I would stop the over water flying and do only domestic ferries, from the Cessna factories in Kansas, back to California. I had put my parents through enough grief. With that decision made, I advised Earl and Bruce that I would only be doing domestic trips from then on.

Shortly after my return, Earl gave me copies of the photos he had taken during his 'fly-bys' immediately after my ditching. I had the idea to have the photo showing me in the raft, still next to my upside-down airplane, enlarged and framed. I hadn't had the opportunity to formally express my appreciation to the Soviet Captain and wanted to send him a 'thank you' letter along with the framed photo. Trouble was, I only had the name of the ship, where it was based and the date of the event to go by. I decided to send the letter and photo, along with another letter of explanation, to the Soviet Embassy in Washington, DC, asking them to forward my 'thank you' letter and the photo to the Captain.

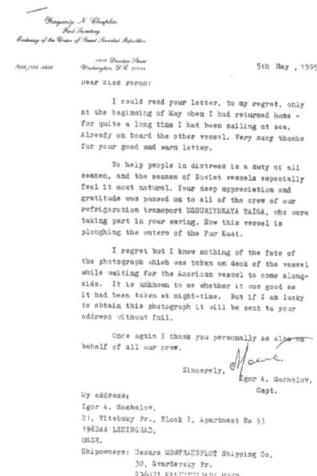

*Letter received from Captain of Soviet vessel through
Soviet Embassy*

I never did receive a reply from the Embassy, but nine months later, I received a heartfelt letter from the Captain of the Soviet rescue ship. No mention was made of the framed photo I had sent, but his response just reinforced what I had felt while onboard his vessel, that no matter the politics, most people will come to the aid of someone in distress.

I had been home about a week when I received a call from the office of VP-91 at Moffett Field, in the South Bay. It was a joint civil-military airport and was the home of the P-3 unit that played such an important role in my rescue. Their unit was called the Stingers; their motto, On Top, On Time, On Target. They wanted to know if I would be interested in coming to Moffett for a ceremony honoring me for how I handled the experience I had in the Pacific.

I was flabbergasted. It was all of them that should get the honor, not me. How could I refuse?

I was to report to Moffett Field that coming Sunday morning, and I could bring my family and several friends to attend. Of course, I'd have to make a speech. *Eee Gads!* And to top it off, it would be televised for the local evening news. Here we go again! I spent the next few sleepless nights trying to come up with an appropriate speech.

The morning of the ceremony was an idyllic summer day in the Bay Area, upper 70s, clear skies, and just a slight breeze. I was expecting the ceremony to take place in a large conference room, or maybe a small auditorium, but when we arrived, we were ushered to the flight line where there were chairs set up for not only me and my family and friends, but also for the senior officers of the airbase. Off to the side was the P-3, tail number 150527, that I had last seen as it made its final pass over my little yellow raft. In front of the airplane was the crew, the same ones that had been flying on that fateful day. They were lined up, at attention. I got a lump in my throat at the sight of them.

Citation ceremony Moffett Field, VP-91 Squadron

The commanding officer of the unit, Dan Baldwin, made a speech detailing the events, as they unfolded that day, and then

Captain Bill Piersig got up to say a few words. This was the first time I had seen him, having only heard his voice, the voice that kept me calm when all hell was breaking loose for me from that 'possible Mayday' call I had made. He was exactly as I pictured him; dark hair, kind eyes, mustache, and a crooked smile.

He introduced the crew which stood off to the side. I was surprised to see a few women mixed in amongst the other crew-members. They all looked so smart in their brilliantly white uniforms.

And then, my heart skipped a beat when I was asked to come up to the lectern.

My hands were shaking as I approached Captain Piersig, but he took my hand in a firm handshake, and I couldn't help myself but to throw my arms around him and hug him. Not very professional for the dignified occasion, but I didn't care. He chuckled as he whispered in my ear, "Good to see you, kid."

Aerial photo of VP-91 P-3 Orion over San Francisco Bay

He, and Cmdr. Baldwin, then presented me with an official VP-91 baseball cap, the colors of the Navy, deep royal blue, and canary yellow. Then, two sets of Naval aviator wings, one that could be worn on your chest, and a smaller one for a suit lapel. They also gave me a leather name patch, one that would be attached, via Velcro, to a flight jumpsuit, typically worn during missions.

If that wasn't enough, Cmdr. Baldwin approached the microphone and in his hands was a blue folder, when opened, like a book, portrayed an 8 x 10 color photograph of the P-3 flying off the coast near San Francisco, the Golden Gate Bridge in the background, and on the other side, a Citation from the Navy Department.

COMMANDING OFFICER
PATROL SQUADRON NINETY-ONE
NAVAL AIR STATION
MOFFETT FIELD CALIFORNIA 94035

```
                                         1650
                                         VP-91/00
                                         18 Aug 84

From:   Commanding Officer, Patrol Squadron NINETY-ONE
To:     MS Heide PORCH

Subj:   VP-91 HONORARY "STINGER"

1.  I take great pride in recognizing your outstanding
achievements on 12 August 1984.

2.  While on a solo trans-Pacific flight in a single
engine Cessna 182 you experienced a total engine
failure requiring you to ditch your airplane in the
Pacific Ocean, 600 miles east of Hawaii. Despite over
14 hours of flight in the cramped confines of the
aircraft you demonstrated remarkable professionalism
and courage during the emergency.  By transmitting a
Mayday message and giving your position before the
engine failure, a Patrol Squadron NINETY-ONE P-3 was
able to escort you until you ditched and remain On-Top,
On-Time, and On-Target until help arrived.

3.  For your professionalism, your dedication and your
courage we salute you and designate you an honorary VP-
91 Stinger.

                                  D. W. BALDWIN
```

From: Commanding Officer, Patrol Squadron NINETY-ONE
To: MS Heidi PORCH
Subj: VP-91 HONORARY "STINGER"
1. I take great pride in recognizing your outstanding achievements on 12 August 1984.
2. While on a solo trans-Pacific flight in a single engine Cessna 182 you experienced a total engine failure requiring you to ditch your airplane in the Pacific Ocean, 600 miles east of Hawaii. Despite over 14 hours of flight in the cramped confines of the aircraft you demonstrated remarkable professionalism and courage

during the emergency. By transmitting a Mayday message and giving your position before the engine failure, a Patrol Squadron NINETY-ONE P-3 was able to escort you until you ditched and remain On-Top, On-Time, and On-Target until help arrived.

3. For your professionalism, your dedication, and your courage we salute you and designate you an honorary VP-91 Stinger.

D.W. Baldwin

As I stood there listening to those unbelievable words being spoken, seeing the crewmembers standing at attention, and the look of pride on the face of Bill Piersig, I couldn't help but think of my Dad, and how proud he must have felt at this moment, seeing his little girl, the one that used to perch herself on phone books so she could fly the beloved Cessna 170 decades earlier, become an honorary Naval Aviator.

Receiving honorary Naval Aviator wings from Capt. Bill Piersig

I was grateful for the few minutes it took to shake hands, and wait for the applause coming from everyone to subside. And then it was my turn.

"When I was about to go down, I told you guys that if I ever got out of this mess, the beer was on me," and I reached into a bag I had brought with me to the podium and pulled out a large can of Australian Fosters Beer.

"So, here it is, and a box of straws!"

Mission complete.

Crew of P-3 Orion and Heidi

Thirty-Three

August 2020

I turned to my left and stared out the window from the cockpit of a Delta Air Lines Airbus A330. The nearly 300 passengers in the cabin were probably sleeping, or watching movies, anticipating their arrival into Honolulu in about an hour. We were about 500 miles from Oahu.

From 38,000 feet, the waters of the blue Pacific Ocean below shimmered from the afternoon sunlight, but it was different. I was a pure spectator this time, not a participant.

This was the spot. This is where I experienced one of the best and one of the worst days in my life. I had learned so much about myself. What a gift it had been.

And this is where Bob had his final 'landing.' Could he sense that I was looking down at him? Was Homer able to escape from his perch in the cockpit of the crippled plane, and was he floating somewhere in the Pacific still? Maybe one day he would wash up on the shore of a distant island. I hoped so.

My First Officer broke the silence.

"Captain, I'd like a cup of coffee right about now. You want some?"

"No. But how about I buy you a beer in Honolulu tonight. I'll tell you a story."

Epilogue

When I was a young girl, I had a plan. Nothing panned out the way I had expected, except for the final goal. I did become an airline pilot, but by an unforeseen path, one with experiences I never could have imagined. I was lucky, yes. But luck was only a small part of it. Ever since I could remember, I had visualized what my future would be.

Bob's death triggered in me a search for answers. Why him? He was the expert on overwater flying and survival. Why did I live? I started to read books on religion and metaphysics and the occult. To this day, I am still searching for answers. And so far, the only thing that makes sense to me is that all things are energy. The visualizations I carried with me from a young age were bits of positive energy. Like attracts like. I believe that the energy I put forward eventually came back to me in like measure. Maybe it's what people call 'full circle moments.'

I've had many such moments.

When I was working at the glider port, my friend, John Painter, who was one of the tow pilots and more like a brother to me, also wanted to be an airline pilot. I would pester him relentlessly, telling him that one day I would be his co-pilot for a major airline. I didn't even have a glider license at that point, and there were only a handful of female airline pilots. But John would always humor me and go along with the unlikely premonition.

Years later, thanks to John's intervention with the Chief Pilot at Republic Airlines, I was interviewed and hired as a DC-9 First Officer. Three months later, I flew on John's first flight when he checked out as Captain. My premonition had been fulfilled. Ten years after that, when I had the seniority to become a Captain myself, it was John that acted as my Captain Instructor, and who completed my practical training. In 2017, I flew again with John, as his First Officer, on the wide-body Airbus A-330. It was his retirement flight. Years earlier, the airport commissions had done away with granting a water cannon salute for retiring pilots. But, our friend, Nora Marshall, had connections. So, when we arrived in Seattle on our flight from Amsterdam, John was afforded the experience. As he taxied underneath the shower of water, we looked at each other, appreciating the meaning of the moment.

John Painter's first Captain flight

In the summer of 2000, I was fortunate to become Cruise Captain-qualified on the iconic Boeing 747, with routes throughout Asia and Europe. I had always regretted not being able to become a pilot in the Navy, even though I held an 'honorary' title. So, when Northwest Airlines (Republic Airlines had merged with Northwest Orient) started offering pilots the opportunity to volunteer for military charters to and from Kuwait, Germany, and Italy, I jumped at the chance. It was my small contribution towards supporting our troops and paying respect to my father.

And in a way, I had become a 'military' pilot.

When Delta Air Lines (yes, there was another merger) decided to retire the 747 fleet, I became a Captain on the A-330. On one flight, a little girl came into the cockpit while the passengers were boarding. Her eyes were wide with wonder at the sight of the cockpit. Gone were the analog gauges of previous aircraft. In their place were colorful digital display units; mini-tv screens with symbols and 'hieroglyphics' of aircraft systems that might as well have been a foreign language to a young mind. I let her use the PA to say hello to her parents and announce the flight time to Paris, and could hear applause coming from the cabin.

Upon arrival in Paris, she entered the cockpit again. In her hand was an incredible drawing she had done of the airplane, and me, as seen through one of the windows. My memories flashed back to that little girl who marveled at the pilots and crew on that flight to Detroit, and who sparked in me a lifelong desire to become one of their cadre. Had I done that for her? Did I help her to create a memory that she would remember for the rest of her life? I felt humbled.

Heidi taxiing A330 for takeoff, Portland, OR

Covid forced me into an early retirement. I still had fourteen months of doing a job I loved before my age would require that I put away my epaulets forever. It was a difficult adjustment. Every airline pilot thinks about the day when it will be 'the last flight.' You are able to bring your family members along with you to celebrate the occasion on one of your layovers. The company hangs a large color photograph of the type of plane you are currently flying on the Flight Operations wall, in which your coworkers, friends and peers can sign their best wishes. Someone throws you a retirement party.

Covid robbed me of that.

But evidently, the forces that be knew I wasn't finished yet. About a year later, opportunity unexpectedly fell into my lap.

Captain Heidi Porch, Northwest Airline

One day, my neighbor, Alex, asked me how my work was going.

"Didn't you know? I had to retire last year due to Covid."

"Give me your resumé."

"Why?"

Alex was employed as the private chef for a wealthy couple that had a home in Sonoma Valley. They were looking for a new pilot for their private jet. Would I be interested?

I think I took a full second to think about it. Absolutely!

One month later I was in ground school in Savannah, Georgia, learning to fly a Gulfstream VII-500, one of the most advanced large business jets made.

I was in the air again.

I was home.

Gulfstream VII-500, Santa Rosa Airport

The End

A poem written for Heidi

at Sky Sailing Glider Port

Strong and proud they were
Who flew over the earth,
Sharing with birds
and butterflies
the freedom of God.
I remember the spirit of those aviators
Their reminiscences of adventure
and the memory of a life of love
shared in their company.
It was the communion of animate
and inanimate,
of outspread wings and air –
a delicate celestial consummation.
It was the best I have ever known.

Ken J. Couche

PILOT 'STUFF'

Appendix A : Aircraft Preparation for Overwater Ferry

Appendix B: Ferrying a Cessna 188, Ag Husky (Crop duster)

Appendix C: Challenging Airports

Appendix D: Written Transcript of Bob Grantham's Final Flight

APPENDIX A

Aircraft Preparation for Overwater Ferry

The majority of the aircraft we ferried were brand new from the Cessna factories in Wichita, Kansas. These airplanes typically had between one to two hours of operating time, but there were some that only had 20 minutes of flight time before we would fly them to California. If the plane was picked up at the factory to the north of McConnell Air Force Base, we were required to restrict our initial climb until we were several miles west of the field. Those first few minutes at 200 to 400 feet above the ground could be concerning. Was a rag inadvertently left in the gas tank, were there any loose connections somewhere which would cause the engine to lose power? If so, we would only have seconds to find an appropriate emergency landing site.

The planes would be flown as 'hard' as possible on the way to California. We flew at the lowest legal altitude in order to get as much power on the engine as possible. Every discrepancy that was found, no matter how insignificant, would be noted. The list would be given to maintenance upon arrival in Vacaville, and be rectified before the airplane would be ferried.

Immediately upon arrival in Vacaville, a hot oil sample would be taken from the engine. The sample would be sent to a laboratory for analysis. If any microscopic particles of metal appeared in the sample, a top overhaul would be accomplished. The plane would then be flown for another ten to twenty hours before another analysis could be made to ensure that the engine was in top working order.

For the next two to five days the mechanics would perform the tanking procedure. Carpeting would be removed, as well as the co-pilot seat and rear passenger seats. These would be broken down and stored in plastic bags to be placed in the rear section of the aircraft. For single-engine airplanes, two aluminum fuel tanks would be installed, each one containing between 90 to 137 gallons, depending upon the model of the airplane, as long as they complied with weight and balance restrictions. This would usually give us two-and-a-half-hours of reserve fuel. Most ferry fuel systems incorporated a simple gravity feed operation, although there were a few models of aircraft where the bottom of the ferry tank was below the level of the engine's fuel pump. If that was the case, an electric fuel pump would be installed to pump the last 20 gallons of ferry fuel up into the engine. Once the ferry tanks were installed, the LORAN and HF radios would be installed along with the antennas.

At this point an inspection is made by the FAA to check that the integrity of the aircraft has not been compromised, and that the weight and balance is within proper limits. All of the paperwork is inspected and if everything is in order a ferry permit is issued.

A test flight is now performed to ensure that the fuel system operates normally. Once the aircraft climbs to a safe cruising altitude, utilizing the normal wing fuel tanks, the engine is run off of each ferry tank for two to three minutes. The ferry tank being used is shut off until the engine sputters before switching to the second ferry tank. This ensures that the engine will operate normally off of each tank. In addition to checking the fuel system, the autopilot (if installed), or wing leveler is thoroughly checked. All discrepancies will be reported to maintenance upon landing and will be addressed as this will be the last chance to have problems corrected before departure.

Several hours before an evening departure, the aircraft is

loaded with most of the supplies that will be needed for the flight over water including, a tool kit (normally placed directly beneath the pilot's seat), a four-man life raft (which contains a leak stopper kit, an inflation pump, solar still, fishing kit, sea anchor, whistle, flashlight, signal mirror, small towel, sea dye marker, knife, water bag, first aid kit, solar blanket and one parachute flare), extra survival supplies (life preserver, hand-held radio, ELT, flare gun, food, and anything else the pilot desires), chart case, and a metal trunk used to package the instruments and antennas that were used for the flight.

Once the airplane is loaded, it is taxied to a compass rose that is painted on the asphalt in one of the run-up areas near the runway. In order to navigate accurately, a computation must be done considering the difference between Magnetic North and True North. This is known as the 'variation,' and are portrayed on navigational charts as 'Isogonic Lines' which are lines joining points on the earth's surface at which the magnetic declination is the same. Along with that, compass 'deviations' must also be computed. Objects in the airplane (engine block, radios, portable ELTs) create their own magnetic fields which can affect compass readings. The compass deviations must be checked for every 30 degrees of a 360-degree circle. All of the radios and lights are turned on during this check as it is necessary to place an electrical load upon the aircraft to ensure accuracy. The deviations are plotted on an X-Y graph and should resemble a sine wave. Using this graph, the deviations can be interpolated for any heading. In some cases, deviations can be as much as 12 degrees, but most cases are three to six degrees. In determining the actual heading that the pilot will fly, a simple formula is followed: The line drawn on the chart between two points represents your TRUE heading. Apply the number of degrees of the magnetic VARIATION gives you your MAGNETIC heading. Then, add or subtract the number of degrees of DEVIATION to obtain your COMPASS heading, which is the heading used to navigate. Nearly every new pilot learns this formula by memorizing the following phrase:

<u>T</u>rue <u>V</u>irgins <u>M</u>ake <u>D</u>ull <u>C</u>ompany.

Once the plane is back at the tie-down area of the ramp, the plane is fueled for the overwater flight. Since the aircraft will be over the maximum gross takeoff weight, the tires should be inflated to 150% of the normal pressure (psi) reading. The oil quantity is also checked at this time. When taxiing the aircraft in an overweight condition, care must be taken when making turns to eliminate placing undue sideway stresses to the tires.

A flight plan is now filed over the phone with Oakland Flight Service Station (FSS). An international format is used which includes, in addition to the usual information, a description of the survival equipment on board (color of raft, size, and whether it has a cover), the HF frequencies to be used, and confirming that position reporting will be required every 2½ degrees of longitude. For flight planning purposes, an average true airspeed is computed. Due to the overweight condition of the airplane, the performance will be degraded during the initial portion of the flight until the normal airspeed can be obtained. For example, a Cessna 182 will use 150 kts for the average True Airspeed (TAS). The distance to Honolulu is approximately 2150 nautical miles and the estimated time en route will be 17 hours.

Time to rest. By this time, it is typically around 4:00 pm. The goal is to be able to sleep until 11:00 pm.

That evening, about an hour and a half prior to takeoff, a call is made to the National Weather Service. A request is made to speak to an 'Aviation Weather Specialist.' The briefing includes:

- Low Level Winds Aloft forecast at 5,000 ft and 10,000 ft.
- Overall average wind component (Two to five days prior to departure, the overall wind component is checked to see if a trend is developing which might exceed the maximum headwind that can be accepted and still be able to keep the necessary fuel reserve.)
- Actual winds by zones (California to Hawaii includes eight different zones. Each zone represents approximately 300 miles). Winds will be given in True North

and will have to be converted to Magnetic by subtracting the easterly variation of each zone.

- Any significant weather en route (Rain, thunderstorms, etc.)
- Valid times for the winds.

Once the briefing is complete, calculations are made for what will be the compass headings, time en route, groundspeeds and Equal Time Point, otherwise known as the 'Point of No Return' (the point in the flight plan at which it takes the same amount of time to return to your point of departure, or to continue to your destination). This is the point, if passed, commits you to continue to your destination.

At this point, we would pack any personal items, such as food and drink. Typically, foodstuffs would include limited dehydrated fruits (Jim York discovered the hard way about limiting these fruits. He had recently tried dried prunes and liked them so much that he ate nearly an entire bag on the last leg from Norfolk Island to Sydney. Much to his unwelcome surprise, he developed a severe case of gastrointestinal distress. He finally succumbed to this malady by performing an 'expulsion' of the digested matter into a paper bag, thereby becoming a member of the 'White Bag Club.' Before starting his descent into Sydney, he tossed the offensive parcel out the window. It struck the leading edge of the horizontal stabilizer and exploded. Upon landing in Sydney, we were required to stay inside the cockpit until Immigration and Customs officers approach the plane, hand an aerosol container of disinfectant and insecticide to us through the cracked cockpit window, where we would spray the aerosol and sit there for ten minutes, until we were given permission to exit the aircraft. Needless to say, the officers were perplexed at the rather large amount of 'organic matter' adhering to the edge of the tail. They all looked at Jim with inquisitive looks on their faces. "Bird... *a really big* bird!" was all that Jim could say.

Nuts and some fresh fruits and vegetables were also popular on these long flights. They were a good source for energy.

Something salty would also be consumed, as we would often fly in very warm temperatures and our sweat depleted us of salt. My comrades liked to take large canteens of coffee to help stay awake, but I found that you would come 'off' a caffeine high well before the flight ended, and you would be more tired than if you had not consumed any caffeine in first place.

A final preflight would be accomplished paying close attention to the fuel caps, oil caps and the tire inflation.

Finally, a phone call to Travis Air Force Base would be made to obtain our clearance. Most of the time we would be cleared via the original routing requested in our flight plan, but occasionally a reroute would be given. By calling ATC on the phone, we would have time to do a replotting and recalculations instead of obtaining our clearance once airborne, and dealing with the hassle of trying to do all of the replotting in the confines of the cockpit in the dark.

Typical Flight Plan:

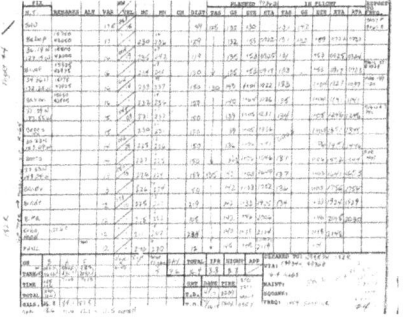

Loran chart detail:

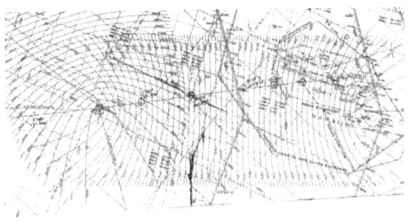

APPENDIX B

Ferrying a Cessna 188, Ag Husky (Crop Duster)

On one occasion, Transair was contracted to ferry an Ag plane from California to Australia. At the time, I was the only ferry pilot available to fly a taildragger. The flight would consist of two planes, a Cessna 188, also known as an Ag Husky, a crop duster, and my wingman, Denny, would fly a Cessna 172.

Tanking a crop duster for overwater flying proved to be a challenge for the maintenance staff. It involved converting the 'hopper,' the chamber that would normally carry the insecticide to be sprayed, into a gas tank. A temporary vacuum system also had to be installed in order to have the necessary instrumentation (Attitude Indicator, Artificial Horizon, Heading Indicator, ADF, VOR, and Turn Coordinator) needed to fly in IFR, instrument flying conditions.

Needless to say, space was extremely limited in the cockpit. There would be no room for the usual radios and supplies normally carried on ferry flights. There was no room for both the LORAN and HF radios. My wingman would have the HF radio for communications for both of us. However, I was able to find a space on a small ledge directly behind the pilot seat for the LORAN. It required me to contort myself like a pretzel in order to use the radio, but it was better than nothing.

The standard cockpit configuration for Ag planes eliminated the need for a conventional floor. While sitting in the pilot seat, you could look straight down and see the control cables for the flight control surfaces, and below that the 'skin' of the belly fuselage. Our mechanic was able to find a couple of plywood boards that could be wedged around the base of the pilot seat. This afforded me a small space to cram a scaled down version of my flight bag (more of a 'pull apart' portfolio case), so I could carry my charts and flight papers. A small canvas tool kit could be placed directly underneath the seat, and my overnight bag and life raft would be wedged directly behind the seat.

This would be the longest ferry flight I had attempted.

Ag Husky being prepped for tanking

Route of flight/flight times:

Vacaville, CA to Hilo, Hawaii: 19 hours
Hilo, Hawaii to Christmas Island, Kiribati: 10 hours
Christmas Island to American Samoa: 11 hours
American Samoa to Nausori, Fiji: 7 hours
Nausori, Fiji to Nadi, Fiji: 1 hour
Nadi, Fiji to Norfolk Island: 10 hours
Norfolk Island to Sydney to Bankstown: 10 hours
Total flight time: 68 hours in six days

Temporary flight and navigation radios

Temporary VOR, ADF and VHF radios

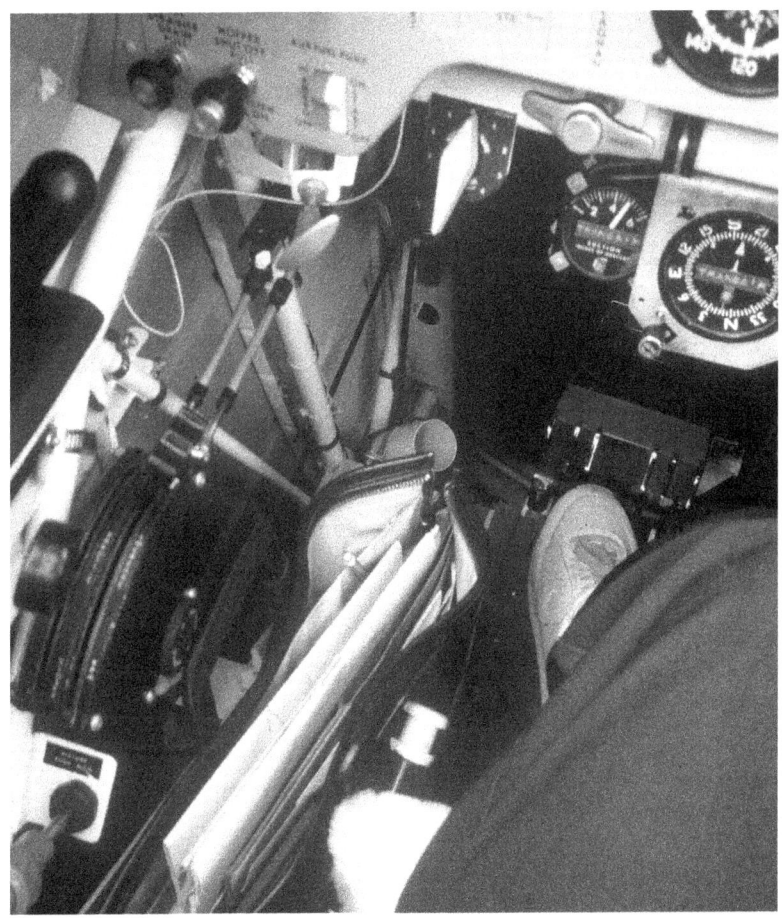

Chart portfolio

What made this trip more challenging was that there would be no autopilot, or wing leveler installed. I would have to hand fly each leg. I decided to make my own version of an autopilot. I found a small bungee cord at the local hardware store. It had hooks at each end. I was able to hook one end to the tube running beneath the forward instrument panel, loop it around the control stick once, and hook the other end to the right side of the instrument panel. This allowed me about 30 seconds of hands-free flying to be able to twist around in my seat, record LORAN readings, and then plot my location. Unfortunately, the cord was just a bit too tight. The tension would pull slightly on the control stick, putting the plane into a shallow descent.

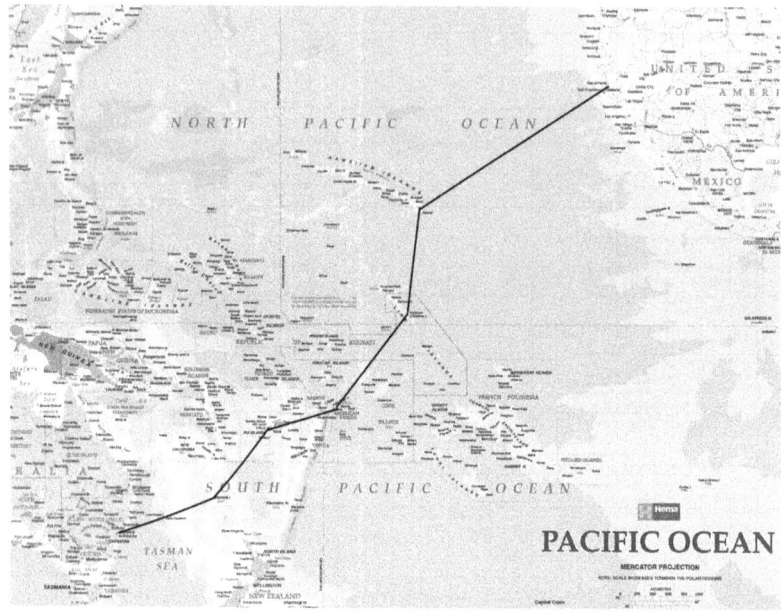

Route of flight

Ag Husky and Cessna 172 at Hilo, Hawaii

Flying under FAR Part 91 regulations did not give us the luxury of any specified required crew rest on our layovers, so boredom and fatigue was definitely something that had to be dealt with. To help counteract this, we used to occasionally fly in formation. The concentration needed to do this usually helped with the monotony of flying for hours on end. The tendency to want to fall asleep was a different matter. I had discovered from previous trips that a wave of sleepiness would usually hit right before sunrise. This 'lull' would last about 15 minutes, and then you would be fairly alert for the next few hours before another wave would hit. Fortunately, the tendency to fall asleep would not last nonstop for the entire duration of the flight.

Flying formation

If the plane had a wing leveler, or autopilot, and a pilot was getting sleepy, he would tell his wingman that he needed to 'doze.' The pilot would turn the volume up all the way on his radio, slide down into his seat and close his eyes. The rest of us (if we were in a group of airplanes) would cease all conversation, and keep a close eye on the pilot trying to rest. If we needed to wake up the pilot, a radio call to him would be so loud that it would awaken him. However, on one particular flight, the pilot not only dozed, but was dead asleep. The only way to arouse him was to have a faster airplane fly underneath his aircraft, and then pull up abruptly once he had overtaken the sleeping pilot's airplane. This usually would cause the plane to fly into the propwash of the passing airplane, and wake him up.

Sometimes, we would play a game of 'Battleship' during our crossings. I had drawn grids onto sheets of paper, each grid containing 100 squares. I'd give a sheet to each pilot before take-off, so each pilot would be able to play. Playing this game was a good way to 'kill' some time.

Flying the Ag plane forced me into coming up with some alternative ways of staying awake. Sometimes, I would intentionally drop a pencil down between my knees. The pencil would drop down to the belly of the aircraft. I would take my shoes and socks off, and attempt to pick up the pencil with my toes. Another time, I took a pair of blunt-nose pliers out of my tool kit and tried to pluck my eyebrows using a small mirror that was also in the tool kit. However, from experiencing this attempt at a beauty regiment, I would not recommend this practice.

We encountered numerous problems on this particular ferry flight. Just a few hours out of California, I discovered that in order to get the ADF, Automatic Direction Finder, to work, I had to turn off the aircraft's alternator. Fortunately, my wingman could do the majority of the navigating, as finding Christmas Island, located in Kiribati, was extremely challenging. The island is only 12 miles long, and 9 miles wide. You had to be nearly on top of it to see it.

Approaching Christmas Island Airport

Christmas Island has a fascinating history. During World War II, the United States Army Air Force used the airport as a refueling stop, as well as a staging point for attacks on the Gilbert Islands, then partially occupied by Japan.

When we were making our approach into Christmas Island, the winds at the airport presented us with a severe crosswind. There is only one asphalt runway, about 2,000 feet in length. We made two attempts at landing, but the winds were just too intense. We had no choice but to land on the taxiway, which had a more complimentary angle to the winds.

Christmas Island Terminal

Our next unexpected roadblock was when we landed in Nausori, in Fiji. After a couple of hours trying to find a hotel room, none were to be found. The last thing I wanted to do was to climb back into the airplane to fly in search of accommodations, but that's what we did. An hour away was the larger town of Nadi, Fiji, and hotel vacancies! Sleep never felt so good.

Only two legs to go. Tomorrow would be the leg to Norfolk Island, and then on to Sydney. About ten minutes out of Fiji, some weather had moved in, and my wingman and I got separated. The weather was not unusually bad, but the clouds were such that we could not keep in visual contact with one another. We had approximately nine hours of flying ahead of us, so the assumption was that we had plenty of time to join up again. Out in the middle of the ocean, the only way you could join up with one another was to describe the shapes of clouds nearby. The problem was, in most cases, the other pilots only saw clouds in the shape of women's body parts! Boys will be boys. I remember on this flight, after trying for hours to join up, I described a cloud in the shape of a French poodle sitting on its haunches. We ended up meeting under the 'jaw.'

When flying in a group, and clouds were encountered, the practice was to stagger your altitude with one another by around five hundred feet, to avoid hitting each other. And it was important for everyone to fly the same heading. Each pilot would take note of the relative position of his comrade. The first pilot entering the clouds would announce, "I'm in." Upon exiting the clouds, the pilot would announce, "I'm clear." He would then look in the area where his wingman should be, and be able to notice as soon as that pilot made an exit out of the clouds.

We successfully arrived at Norfolk Island, and had a leisurely evening visiting with the local friends we had made from our previous flights.

One last sprint the next day to Sydney. What could go wrong?

The next morning would have us flying ten hours before we would be making our approach into Sydney International Airport, doing a quick turnaround with Customs and Immigration, and then the short 25-minute flight to Bankstown, where the Cessna distributor was waiting for us.

Somehow, our estimated time en route was incorrect. We ended up being 40 minutes late entering Australia airspace. We found ourselves being intercepted by a military escort. My wingman took the lead in communicating with the Australian fighter pilot, and after a few tense moments, they were satisfied that a Cessna 172 and Ag plane were no threat to their national security, and allowed us to land in Sydney with no further drama.

Aside from the 'ditching,' this was perhaps the most challenging and fatiguing ferry flight I had made. But my exhaustion immediately melted away when we taxied up to the hangar at

Bankstown. There, all the staff were lined up to congratulate me on being the first woman to deliver an Ag plane to Australia. It was extremely gratifying, but in my mind, once was enough!

APPENDIX C

Challenging Airports

Lord Howe Island:

In thinking back over the varied and unique airports throughout the Pacific we encountered, two come to mind that were particularly challenging; Lord Howe Island and an airport with no name in New Guinea.

Lord Howe was a very small island positioned about halfway between Norfolk Island and the eastern coast of Australia; about 450 miles from each. It is only six miles long and a little over a mile wide. The airport has one runway with a length of around 2,900 feet. Normally this would be plenty long for most airplanes to land upon, but there was a unique characteristic about this particular airport.

The runway ran across the narrowest part of the island. The runway ran in an east/west direction with beaches and water at both ends. To the south of the airport is Mount Gower, an inactive volcano with an elevation of 2,800 feet. To the north of the airport is a smaller hill.

On one particular flight, I was paired up with Eric. We were on the last leg of our trip to Australia, when about three hours into the flight, Eric informed me that he had miscalculated his fuel, and to be on the safe side, we should probably land at Lord Howe to put on some more gas. Normally, this wouldn't have been a problem. Lord Howe had services at the airport, and it would be easy to get in and out. However, Lord

Howe Airport, at that time, had a permanent NOTAM, Notice to Airmen, associated with its airport. In general terms, it stated that in windy conditions, there was moderate to severe turbulence at *both* ends of the runway, and at the same time, severe tailwinds at *both* ends of the runway. Apparently, the prevailing winds would flow around the southern face of Mount Gower, and create eddies and turbulence on the downwind side of the mountain, right where the runway was situated.

Approaching Lord Howe Island

Pilots always want to land into the wind. It provides the best performance, and the shortest landing distance. So, even though a 2,800-foot runway seemed more than long enough, landing in turbulence with a tailwind could eat up most of the runway, and then you were going to end up in the water at the end of the runway.

Eric assured me that we didn't have a choice. He needed the fuel. I couldn't continue on to Sydney by myself, as we had filed our flight plan as a 'flight' of two. However, I selfishly volunteered Eric to go first for a landing.

As I circled offshore, I could hear that Eric had to 'go-around' and abort his first attempt at landing. He made it on his second attempt.

It was my turn. I carried a little extra airspeed to compensate for the turbulence, and as I flew the last thousand feet of the approach, aiming for the touchdown point on the runway, it felt as though I was in a washing machine. Everything loose was flying around the cockpit, and it was difficult to read the instruments with all of the jostling I was experiencing.

I landed a bit long, and could feel the unusual sensation of having a tailwind push me along the runway. Suddenly, that 2,800-foot runway looked to be about 800 feet long. The beach and water at the far end of the runway was coming up fast. Then, WHAM! It felt as though I had hit an imaginary brick wall. What were tailwinds at the first half of the runway had turned into a hellacious headwind for the second half. I imagined that this was what it must feel like to land on the bucking deck of an aircraft carrier, and your tailhook catches the wire in order to stop you. Well, maybe not like that exactly, but my heart was pounding like it was.

Overhead view of Lord Howe Airport

Once Eric refueled, the takeoff was nearly as exciting, but we knew what to expect.

That was my one, and only, time flying into Lord Howe. I vowed, never again.

New Guinea:

This 'airport,' and I use the word lightly, was one my friend, Jim York, experienced when he delivered a Cessna 185 to New Guinea.

The buyer of the plane happened to be a missionary pilot, using the airplane to deliver supplies into remote areas of the island. He had been waiting anxiously for this new airplane to arrive. After Jim had turned over all of the paperwork to the new owner, Jim discovered that his flight back home had been cancelled. The next available flight to the States would be in three days.

The new owner invited Jim to accompany him on his 'rounds' the following day. Jim was always up for an adventure, and so he accepted.

They planned to fly to four different locations; most of them nothing more than a grass strip or a gravel runway, with no services. You were on your own.

Dirt runway, New Guinea

Their last stop of the day was in an area of the island of lush tropical foliage and lots of mountains. There were no roads that Jim could see. Jim was expecting to pass over these mountains to a clearing where the airport must be, but instead, the pilot said, "There it is straight ahead."

"Where?" Jim asked.

"There!" and the pilot pointed to a mountain top where a small church stood.

The 'runway' was hard-packed dirt, and could not have been more than 600-700 feet long. It was on an extremely steep slope, where a church stood at the end of the runway, on the apex of the hill.

As they made the approach, the pilot informed Jim that the runway was so steep, that when you touched down, you'd have to add full power in order to make it to the top of the hill. And it is so steep that you can't even see the buildings at the top when you first touchdown.

Approaching mountain top runway, New Guinea

Jim told me that he almost peed his pants. And he was fearless!

Final Approach, New Guinea

Departing was just as exciting.

The pilot held the brakes, ran the engine up to full power, released the brakes, and bounced down the hillside. At the end, there still wasn't enough speed to lift off, so the plane just 'fell' off the end of the runway into the ravine until there was enough lift to climb out of the canyon. I'm sure Jim was 'finding God.'

Better him, than me.

Departing view, New Guinea

APPENDIX D

Written Transcript of Bob Grantham's Final Flight

BOB GRANTHAM - RUBBER DUCK
LAST FERRY FLIGHT
09 DEC 1982

The following is a written transcript of Aeronautical Radio, Inc., San Francisco
Communication Center recorded communications relating to trouble experienced by
N74957 of December 9, 1982. The aircraft, registered to Brents International of
Alameda, CA apparently ditched somewhere in the Pacific. This transcript covers
the period 0850 thru 1028 GMT.

0850:19   SAN FRANCISCO NOVEMBER SEVEN FOUR NINE FIVE SEVEN ON FIVE SIX

0850:25   WHO'S CALLING SAN FRANCISCO

0850:28   ROGER NOVEMBER SEVEN FOUR NINE FIVE SEVEN. WAS TWO NINER THREE ZERO NORTH
          ONE FOUR TWO THREE FIVE WEST AT ZERO EIGHT FOUR NINER SIX THOUSAND ESTIMATING
          CITTA ZERO NINER FIVE ZERO AND A REQUEST

0850:47   AH SAY YOU'RE VERY VERY WEAK WHAT IS YOUR LATITUDE - PRESENT LATITUDE

0850:52   TWO NINER THREE ZERO NORTH

0850:56   TWO NINE ZERO - TWO NINE THREE ZERO NORTH ONE FOUR TWO THREE FIVE WEST, YOUR
          FLIGHT LEVEL.

0851:01   SIX THOUSAND

0851:08   OKAY, NOW GIVE ME YOUR ESTIMATED POSITION. YOU'RE VERY WEAK.

0851:12   CITTA, THATS CHARLIE INDIA TANGO TANGO ALPHA ZERO NINER FIVE ZERO

0851:18   OKAY YOU SAY YOU HAVE A REQUEST

0851:20   THATS AFIRMATIVE. IF I COULD CONTACT HONOLULU I NEED TO PASS IT TO HIM. WE'RE
          HAVING A SLIGHT PROBLEM AND I NEED THE COAST GUARD TO BE NOTIFIED. I'D LIKE
          AN ESCORT IF POSSIBLE. ALSO FOR SAN FRANCISCO I'D LIKE FOR YOU TO CALL THE
          LOCAL ALAMEDA NUMBER. IT IS AREA CODE FOUR ONE FIVE FIVE TWO ONE ZERO SEVEN
          EIGHT TWO ANYONE THAT ANSWERS - A MISTER ED THERRIEN SHOULD ANSWER. THATS
          TANGO HOTEL ECHO ROMEO ROMEO INDIA ECHO NOVEMBER ADVISE HIM WE ARE LOSING
          OIL PRESSURE ON THE LEFT ENGINE. ANTICIPATE WILL HAVE TO SHUT IT DOWN WITHIN
          THE HOUR

0852:09   OKAY SAY AGAIN THE MAN'S NAME

0852:12   THATS THERRIEN TANGO HOTEL ECHO ROMEO ROMEO INDIA ECHO NOVEMBER AND YOU CAN
          TELL HIM THE OIL PRESSURE IS DOWN TO FORTY FIVE PSI. IT IS GRADUALLY DROPPING
          AND AS I SAID WE ANTICIPATE SHUTTING DOWN WITHIN THE HOUR.

0852:30   OKAY THE OIL PRESSURE IS DOWN TO FORTY FIVE PSI AND REPEAT YOUR REMARKS AGAIN
          ABOUT YOU WANT THE COAST GUARD TO BE NOTIFIED AND YOU WANT - YOU MIGHT WANT -
          AH YOU DO WANT AN ESCORT IN

0852:43   WELL WE CAN HOLD OFF HERE A LITTLE BIT. WE'D LIKE TO HAVE THEM NOTIFIED THAT
          WE ANTICIPATING A PROBLEM HERE. IF THIS OIL PRESSURE DROPS ANY FURTHER I'LL

HAVE TO SHUT IT DOWN BUT I WOULD LIKE YOU TO HAVE THEM ON ALERT SO THEY KNOW THAT AH THEY CAN COME OUT OF BARBERS POINT AND MEET US

0853:04 OKAY I'M GONNA READ YOU BACK WHAT I GOT HERE. REQUESTING THE COAST GUARD BE NOTIFIED YOU ANTICIPATE A PROBLEM AND AH YOU WANT THEM TO BE ON ALERT THE NUMBER FOUR ONE FIVE FIVE TWO ONE OH SEVEN EIGHT TWO ADVISE THEM YOU'RE LOSING OIL PRESSURE ON LEFT ENGINE AH WILL HAVE TO SHUT IT DOWN WITHIN THE HOUR AND FOR MISTER THERRIEN THE OIL PRESSURE IS DOWN TO FORTY FIVE PSI. GO AHEAD

0853:26 THATS AFFIRMATIVE WE ANTICIPATE SHUTTING IT DOWN WITHIN THE HOUR AH IT MAY LAST A LITTLE BIT FURTHER AH AH BUT WE ARE HAVING A PROBLEM AND WE NEED THEM NOTIFIED

0853:37 OKAY AH ROGER ROGER AH I'LL PASS THIS ON TO ATC AH MAINTAIN A LISTENING WATCH ON THIS FREQUENCY OKAY

0853:46 THATS AFFIRMATIVE ALSO WOULD YOU REVISE OUR TRUE AIR SPEED TO ONE SIX FIVE KNOTS WE PULLED THE POWER BACK TO TRY TO SAVE THIS ENGINE

0853:54 YOUR TRUE AIR SPEED IS WHAT

0853:56 ONE SIX FIVE

0853:58 ONE SIXTY FIVE YOUR TRUE AIR SPEED DO YOU HAVE DO YOU HAVE A SELCAL

0854:03 THATS NEGATIVE I'LL MAINTAIN LISTENING WATCH

0854:05 YES SIR MAINTAIN LISTENING WATCH AND I'LL BE AH I'M SURE I'LL BE BACK WITH YOU IN A COUPLE MINUTES

0854:10 THANK YOU SIR

0900:20 NOVEMBER SEVEN FOUR NINE FIVE SEVEN SAN FRANCISCO

0900:24 NINE FIVE SEVEN GO AHEAD

0900:26 YEAH ATC WANTS A FIRST OF ALL THEY WANT YOUR AH YOUR FUEL ON BOARD

0900:31 OKAY STANDBY RIGHT NOW I'VE GOT AH (pause) ABOUT SEVEN HOURS AND FORTY FIVE MINUTES ENDURANCE QQQ (garble)

0900:50 I'M SORRY YOU'RE A LITTLE HARD TO READ SAY AGAIN

0900:52 SEVEN PLUS FOUR FIVE

0900:55 SEVEN PLUS FOUR FIVE FUEL ON BOARD HOW MANY SOULS INCLUDING YOURSELF

0900:59 AH TWO

0901:01 AH TWO THERES TWO PEOPLE ON BOARD INCLUDING YOURSELF CORRECT

0901:03   THAT'S AFFIRMATIVE

0901:05   OKAY WE'LL BE BACK WITH YOU

0901:06   ROGER

0910:54   HONOLULU NOVEMBER SEVEN FOUR NINE FIVE SEVEN ON FIVE SIX

0910:59   NOVEMBER NINE - SEVEN FOUR NINE FIVE SEVEN HONOLULU GO AHEAD

0911:01   ROGER SIR AH YOU CAN STILL GO AHEAD AND HAVE THE COAST GUARD COME OUT FOR
           AN INTERCEPT MY OIL PRESSURE HAS JUST DROPPED ANOTHER POUND OR TWO AND I
           DON'T KNOW THE EXACT TIME I'M GONNA BE ABLE TO SHUT THIS ENGINE DOWN BUT
           MIGHT AS WELL GET THE COAST GUARD OUT LOOKIN FOR ME

0911:20   OKAY YOUR AH YOUR OIL PRESSURE HAS DROPPED A POUND OR TWO AND YOU DON'T
           KNOW WHAT TIME YOU'RE GONNA SHUT THE ENGINE DOWN. WANT THE COAST GUARD
           INTERCEPT. STANDBY

0911:31   ROGER

0913:14   NOVEMBER SEVEN FOUR NINE FIVE SEVEN SAN FRANCISCO

0913:20   NINE FIVE SEVEN GO AHEAD

0913:21   YEAH ATC WANTS TO KNOW IF YOU ARE DECLARING AN EMERGENCY

0913:25   THAT'S AFFIRMATIVE I'D LIKE COAST GUARD INTERCEPT

0913:28   OKAY THANK YOU

0931:28   NOVEMBER SEVEN FOUR NINE FIVE SEVEN HONOLULU

0931:33   NINE FIVE SEVEN GO AHEAD

0931:35   ROGER HOW DO YOU READ ME ON FIVE SIX

0931:38   ABOUT FOUR BY FOUR

0931:40   YOU'RE VERY WEAK HERE AND HARD TO READ AH WOULD YOU TRY ME ON THREE FOUR
           SIX SEVEN THIRTY FOUR SIXTY SEVEN PLEASE

0931:47   I'D SURE LIKE TO BUT I DON'T HAVE THAT ONE

0931:51   OKAY WHAT FIVE MEG FREQUENCY DO YOU HAVE

0931:55   THIRTEEN THREE HUNDRED IS THE BEST I CAN DO FOR YOU

0931:59   OKAY DO YOU HAVE FIVE FIVE FIVE FOUR

0932:02   LET ME CHECK (pause) NEGATIVE ON FIVE FIVE FIVE FOUR

0932:16   OKAY DO YOU HAVE ANY TWO MEG FREQUENCIES

- 4 -

0932:18   NEGATIVE

0932:20   UNDERSTAND NEGATIVE TWO MEGS

0932:22   THAT'S AFFIRMATIVE

0932:24   ROGER AH STANDBY

0932:28   HONOLULU IF YOU'RE HAVING ANY PROBLEMS READING HIM HERE I'M READING HIM LOUD AND CLEAR I CAN HELP YOU

0932:32   OKAY SAN FRAN AH NOVEMBER SEVEN FOUR NINE FIVE SEVEN REMAIN ON FIVE SIX ZERO THREE PRIMARY

0932:39   NINE FIVE SEVEN

0947:36   HONOLULU NOVEMBER SEVEN FOUR NINE FIVE SEVEN POSITION ON FIVE SIX

0947:40   NOVEMBER SEVEN FOUR NINER FIVE SEVEN HONOLULU GO AHEAD

0947:44   ROGER CITTA ZERO NINER FOUR SIX SIX THOUSAND ESTIMATING TWO SEVEN ZERO SEVEN NORTH ONE FOUR SEVEN THREE ZERO WEST ONE ZERO FOUR FIVE

0947:58   NOVEMBER SEVEN FOUR NINER FIVE SEVEN HONOLULU ROGER

0951:41   NOVEMBER SEVEN FOUR NINER FIVE SEVEN HONOLUL'J

0951:50   NINE FIVE SEVEN GO AHEAD

0951:51   ROGER AH ATC REQUESTS TO KNOW COLOR OF AIRCRAFT THE COLOR OF RAFT AND ANY ADVISE IF YOU HAVE ANY SURVIVAL EQUIPMENT. REQUEST FROM COAST GUARD. GO AHEAD

0952:08   ROGER THE AIRCRAFT IS BEIGE WITH BROWN AND ORANGE TRIM THERES ONE FOUR MAN RAFT ORANGE COLORED OR ORANGE COVERED THE RAFT IS YELLOW. THERES LIFE PRESERVERS EACH PERSON AND FLARES ELT CAPABILITY ON ONE TWO THREE DECIMAL FIVE AND TWO CORRECTION ONE TWO ONE DECIMAL FIVE AND TWO FOUR THREE

0952:39   AH YOUR AIRCRAFT IS BEIGE WITH BROWN AND ORANGE TRIM YOU HAVE ONE ORANGE FOUR MAN RAFT MISSED SOMETHING IN BETWEEN THERE AND YOU HAVE FLARES ELT CAPABILITY AND GIVE ME THE FREQUENCY OF THAT

0953:00   OKAY ONE TWENTY ONE FIVE AND TWO FORTY THREE

0953:03   OKAY ONE TWO ONE FIVE AND AH TWO FOUR AH TWO FOUR ZERO THREE

0953:10   TWO FOUR THREE POINT ZERO THATS UHF

0953:13   TWO FOUR THREE POINT ZERO ROGER AND A WHAT DID YOU HAVE AFTER YOUR ONE ORANGE FOUR MAN RAFT AND YOUR FLARES GO AHEAD

0953:24   OKAY THE RAFT IS YELLOW THE COVER IS ORANGE

0953:27   OKAY THE RAFT IS YELLOW AND THE COVER ORANGE

0953:34   AFFIRMATIVE AND THIS IS ALL ON FILE AT OAKLAND FLIGHT SERVICE IF THEY WANT TO CHECK WITH THEM

0953:40   OKAY WILL ADVISE

1004:47   HONOLULU NOVEMBER SEVEN NINE AH SEVEN FOUR NINE FIVE SEVEN ON FIVE SIX

1004:54   NOVEMBER SEVEN FOUR NINER FIVE SEVEN HONOLULU GO AHEAD

1004:58   OKAY SIR WE SHUT NUMBER ONE ENGINE DOWN UNABLE TO MAINTAIN SIX THOUSAND FEET NOW QQQ (garble) WHAT ALTITUDE I CAN HOLD

1005:04   OKAY YOU SHUT NUMBER ONE ENGINE DOWN AND UNABLE SIX THOUSAND YOU WANT TO KNOW WHAT ALTITUDE YOU CAN HOLD

1005:12   I'LL TELL YOU WHAT I CAN HOLD

1005:13   OKAY AH SIR

1008:58   NOVEMBER SEVEN FOUR NINE FIVE SEVEN HONOLULU

1009:04   GO AHEAD

1009:10   NOVEMBER SEVEN FOUR NINE FIVE SEVEN HONOLULU

1009:12   NINE FIVE SEVEN GO AHEAD

1009:16   HONOLULU YOU NOT READING THE FLIGHT I'VE GOT HIM HERE IF YOU DON'T

1009:20   OKAY I CAN'T READ HIM NOW. ATC IS REQUESTING THE WEATHER CONDITIONS (pause) NOVEMBER SEVEN FOUR NINE FIVE SEVEN HONOLULU I CAN'T READ YOU TOO WELL HERE IF YOU READ ATC REQUESTS WEATHER CONDITIONS WOULD YOU TRANSMIT AND SAN FRANCISCO WILL COPY

1009:38   OKAY RIGHT NOW I CAN SEE THE STARS IT LOOKS LIKE THERE MIGHT BE A LAYER A BROKEN LAYER BENEATH ME AT PROBABLY THREE THOUSAND FEET PRESENT TIME I'M CRUISING THREE THOUSAND FEET

1009:52   OKAY HE SAYS HE CAN SEE THE STARS HE'S GOT BROKEN LAYER BELOW AND HE'S AT ZERO HE'S AT THREE THOUSAND FEET

1010:02   HONOLULU SAN FRANCISCO YOU COPY

1010:04   YEAH HE'S AH HE CAN SEE THE STARS BROKEN LAYER BELOW AND HE'S AT THREE THOUSAND

1010:10   THATS CORRECT ANYTHING ELSE

1010:12   THATS IT FOR NOW

1010:14   OKAY

1010:15   THANK YOU

1012:11 NOVEMBER SEVEN FOUR NINE FIVE SEVEN SAN FRANCISCO

1012:18 NINE FIVE SEVEN GO AHEAD

1012:20 YES SIR HOW FAR AH WHAT IS YOUR ENDURANCE

1012:25 STANDBY RIGHT NOW I FIGURE I GOT ABOUT EIGHT HOURS ENDURANCE

1012:30 YOU GOT ABOUT EIGHT HOURS

1012:32 EIGHT NINE HOURS YEAH

1012:36 OKAY DO YOU KNOW APPROXIMATELY AS CLOSE AS YOU CAN FIGURE HOW MANY MILES FROM HONOLULU YOU ARE

1012:41 STANDBY I'M TAKIN A FIX RIGHT NOW

1012:43 OKAY

1015:14 SAN FRANCISCO NOVEMBER SEVEN FOUR FIVE NINE FIVE SEVEN

1015:18 ROGER GO AHEAD

1015:20 ROGER UNLESS MY LORAN'S LYING TO ME I'M FIVE HUNDRED AND THIRTY ONE MILES FROM HONOLULU AND ABOUT TWENTY MILES LEFT OF TRACK

1015:32 OKAY YOUR AH YOU'RE FIVE HUNDRED AND THIRTY ONE MILES FROM HONOLULU AND TWENTY MILES LEFT OF TRACK CORRECT

1015:39 THATS WHAT MY LORAN SHOWS ME RIGHT NOW. I'M NOT GETTING A AH A GOOD READING ON THE LORAN SO IT MAY BE INACCURATE. I MAY BE A LITTLE BIT CLOSER IN AND A LITTLE BIT CLOSER TO TRACK

1015:49 OKAY THANK YOU

1017:22 OKAY NOVEMBER SEVEN FOUR NINE FIVE SEVEN SAN FRANCISCO

1017:30 NINE FIVE SEVEN GO AHEAD

1017:32 YES SIR WE HAVE YOUR COMPANY ON THE PHONE HERE WE'RE RELAYING ALL THAT INFORMATION TO HIM. HE WANTS TO KNOW IF YOU THINK YOU'RE GONNA MAKE HONOLULU

1017:40 WE'RE DAMN SURE GONNA TRY IT TELL HIM. I'M NOT GONNA GIVE UP THE GHOST TIL I GOTTA GET WET. I HAD TO SHUT THIS ENGINE DOWN THE OIL PRESSURE WAS DOWN TO FORTY TWO PSI THE MANIFOLD PRESSURE WAS FALLING I HAD NO CHOICE BUT TO SHUT IT DOWN. WE'RE HOLDING TWO THOUSAND FEET RIGHT NOW AND EVERYTHINGS GOING ALL RIGHT

1017:59 SAY YOU'RE DOWN TO TWO THOUSAND FEET NOW

1018:01 THATS AFFIRMATIVE

1018:05   OKAY AND YOUR AH OIL PRESSURE IS FORTY TWO PSI AND YOUR MANIFOLD PRESSURE
           IS FALLING AND YOU'RE DOWN TO TWO THOUSAND FEET CORRECT

1018:13   NEGATIVE THAT WAS THE BAD ENGINE THAT WE HAD TO SHUT DOWN. THE OIL PRES-
           SURE WAS DOWN TO FORTY TWO POUNDS AND THE MANIFOLD PRESSURE WAS FALLING
           OFF SO I SHUT IT DOWN, WE'RE RUNNING ON THE RIGHT ENGINE RIGHT NOW IT'S
           LOOKING GOOD AND WE'RE MAINTAINING ABOUT A HUNDRED AND TWENTY FIVE MILES
           AN HOUR WHICH WORKS OUT TO ABOUT A HUNDRED AND TWELVE KNOTS AT TWO THOUSAND
           FEET

1018:36   OKAY YOU'RE AH HUNDRED THEN - YOUR AH YOU'RE MAINTAINING A HUNDRED AND
           TWENTY FIVE MILES AN HOUR AND HOW MANY KNOTS

1018:42   IT WORKS OUT TO ABOUT A HUNDRED AND TWELVE KNOTS

1018:44   A HUNDRED AND TWELVE KNOTS YOU DID SHUT DOWN THE ENGINE AND THE RIGHT
           ENGINE IS RUNNING PRETTY GOOD. CORRECT

1018:49   THATS AFFIRMATIVE

1019:14   OKAY SEVEN FOUR NINE FIVE SEVEN SAN FRANCISCO

1019:19   NINE FIVE SEVEN GO AHEAD

1019:21   OKAY YEAH THEY WANTED TO KNOW WE GOT HIM ON THE PHONE HE WANTS TO KNOW
           THE CONDITION OF THE ENGINE

1019:27   WHICH ENGINE THE GOOD ONE OR THE BAD ONE-

1019:29   THE BAD ONE

1019:31   IT'S SHUT DOWN THE OIL PRESSURE WAS DROPPING OFF IT DROPPED DOWN TO FORTY
           CORRECTION THIRTY SEVEN PSI THE MANIFOLD PRESSURE COULD NOT MAINTAIN
           BUT APPROXIMATELY TWENTY SEVEN INCHES AND IT WAS FALLING AND I SHUT
           IT DOWN AND ITS NOT ON FIRE THE OIL PRESSURE DID NOT GO TO ZERO OR
           ANYTHING LIKE THAT I JUST SHUT IT DOWN.

1019:59   OKAY ROGER THANKYOU

1027:46   HONOLULU NOVEMBER SEVEN FOUR NINE FIVE SEVEN ON FIVE SIX

1027:51   NOVEMBER SEVEN FOUR NINE FIVE SEVEN HONOLULU GO AHEAD

1027:55   OKAY WE'RE AT FIVE HUNDRED FEET BARELY MAINTAINING KEEP YOU ADVISED

1028:00   ROGER HONOLULU YOU'RE AT FIVE HUNDRED FEET BARELY MAINTAINING

I hereby certify that the foregoing transcript is, to the best of my ability, an
accurate copy of all recordings made in the ARINC San Francisco Communication Center
on December 9, 1982, pertaining to N74957 while experiencing engine difficulties.

Raymond A. Lash
Operations Chief

Acknowledgments

This book was decades in the making. For years, I have shared my story with friends and coworkers. The usual response I would get is, "You've got to write a book." I just thought they were being polite. My life experiences did not seem that special to me, but I guess everything is relative. It wasn't until I did a YouTube interview about my experience on the channel FlyWire by Scott Perdue, and I read the hundreds of comments, that I discovered that many of them wanted to know where they could find the book.

I procrastinated for years imagining how difficult writing a book would be. I envisioned my office floor scattered with index cards describing what each chapter would be. I broke into a cold sweat when I realized that I couldn't remember how to use quotation marks. And I must be the 'Queen of Commas.' I finally realized that I just had to sit down and start writing. I was amazed when the words began to flow. Memories came flooding back to me and added depth and meaning to my simple words.

But I could not have completed the process without the support and encouragement from my friends. Many of them became my pseudo-editors, and their feedback was priceless. So, to Captain Steve Foster, Christine Musson, Chris Tack, Nora Marshall, Jen Powers, Barney and Steven Locke my sincere thanks. Your suggestions were invaluable and much appreciated. A very special thank you to my 'literary Guardian Angel,' Karlene Petitt, for setting me on the correct path. Her generous efforts to guide me through this process made my manuscript so much more personal and meaningful. To Nathan Everett, thank you for taking me on, and making the manuscript look like it was written by a professional. And what a gift to have found Alicia Buelow as my graphic designer. She encapsulated the varied elements of my story and transformed them into a moving and descriptive work of art for the cover.

To my 'cheerleaders:' Sydnie Kohara, Robin Lester, Randy Fogerty, Mike Jones, Kathy Pavelko, Ann Hogan, John and Jean Painter, Jack and Karen Gilbert, Angie Accettura, Jack and Lolo Chambers, Jeff and Connie Stocks, Tom and Cat Eckert, Nancy and Warren Fine, my heartfelt thanks. You have always buoyed me up when I doubted my capabilities and needed encouragement. Your friendships are my life's treasures.

My parents, Doug and Gloria, have passed on, but I need to thank them for raising me with the belief that I could do anything, be anything. I know that they were always proud of me, and that is a precious gift to give to a child.

To my sister, Allison Porch. Your love is boundless, and I would not have been able to get through life's difficulties without that love.